We Fought at Kohima

Kohima

A Veteran's Account

Raymond Street
with Robert Street

Pen & Sword
MILITARY

First published in Great Britain by
PEN AND SWORD MILITARY
an imprint of
Pen and Sword Books Ltd
47 Church Street
Barnsley
South Yorkshire S70 2AS

Copyright © Raymond Street with Robert Street, 2015

ISBN 978 1 47384 367 7

The right of Raymond Street with Robert Street to be identified
as the authors of this work has been asserted by them in
accordance with the Copyright, Designs and Patents Act 1988.

A CIP record for this book is available from the British Library.

Printed and bound in England by
CPI Group (UK) Ltd, Croydon, CR0 4YY

Typeset in Times by CHIC GRAPHICS

Pen & Sword Books Ltd incorporates the imprints of
Archaeology, Atlas, Aviation, Battleground, Discovery,
Family History, History, Maritime, Military, Naval, Politics,
Railways, Select, Social History, Transport, True Crime,
Claymore Press, Frontline Books, Leo Cooper, Praetorian Press,
Remember When, Seaforth Publishing and Wharncliffe.

For a complete list of Pen and Sword titles please contact
Pen and Sword Books Limited
47 Church Street, Barnsley, South Yorkshire, S70 2AS, England
E-mail: enquiries@pen-and-sword.co.uk
Website: www.pen-and-sword.co.uk

Contents

Preface

'What did Granddad do in the War?' Many children ask that nowadays. Many parents do not know. Some never found out, because the suffering and the horrors they experienced prevented men talking about their war years. In some cases the details have been taken to their graves. It was the norm to sweep such things under the carpet. I remember my father, Raymond Street, was told on numerous occasions not to 'go on about the war'. It almost became a forbidden subject. Fortunately, my children's grandfather did 'go on', and his story was published in 1998 in a book called *A Brummie in Burma*. It told of his experiences as a typical inner city lad thrust into the amazing sights of exotic foreign lands and into the horrors of war. It chronicled the activities and achievements of his regiment, the 4th Battalion of the Queen's Own Royal West Kents, in India and Burma, including its remarkable defence during the siege of Kohima, where a possible Japanese advance to India was halted.

Subsequent to the publication of that book, many former Royal West Kents contacted me with previously unknown information about the battle, some of which had not even been disclosed to their family or friends. Since then I have researched the siege and taken accounts from those who were there. Unfortunately, memories have sometimes faded, but often they are still vivid.

The present book, whilst dealing with a much wider time period, describes in detail the experiences of the 4th Battalion of the Queen's Own Royal West Kent Regiment during the siege and defence of Kohima. It tells of personal experiences and the individual thoughts of the men as some 446 'West Kents', together with the supporting Assam Regiment and Assam Rifles, held nearly 15,000 Japanese soldiers at bay for sixteen days until relief arrived. Although this was one of the most important land battles of the Second World War, a major turning point in favour of the Allies, it went somewhat unnoticed in the bigger picture. Indeed, those involved in Kohima and the subsequent advance into Burma have become known as 'the Forgotten Army'. Well, many of those involved have told me that they refuse to be forgotten and have freely given me details of their experiences so that the truth may be known once and for all. Their story is told by me in the form of a first-person account by my father, Raymond Street, who even today has vivid memories of that time, and it gives a detailed account of day-to-day events. The story may be disjointed in parts, where recollections of exact events are sometimes unclear, but it has been left this way deliberately, since to resort to invention would detract from these men's achievements.

AT KOHIMA IN APRIL 1944, THE JAPANESE INVASION OF INDIA WAS HALTED

These words are inscribed on the 161st Brigade memorial at Kohima. This was a small garrison town in Nagaland near the Indo-Burmese border. It was a supply depot and convalescent camp on the main road between Imphal and Dimapur, where the British had set up command posts and supply bases. If the Japanese had taken these two towns they would have opened a gateway to invade India; and once they had possession of the associated airstrips and railheads they might have been impossible to stop. Attacks on Imphal and Dimapur were therefore expected, but to get to Dimapur through Kohima, the enemy would have to bring their army over inhospitable, mountainous jungle terrain. The British military authorities did not think this possible. However, despite the jungle conditions and disease, the Japanese did bring over 15,000 men together with their equipment, living off the land and capturing provisions as they went. They headed for Dimapur, but first they had to take Kohima, garrisoned at that time by the Indian Assam Regiment and the 3rd Assam Rifles. At the end of March 1944, the 4th Battalion of the Queen's Own Royal West Kent regiment was sent to help. Just 446 officers and men arrived on 5 April 1944, to fight at Kohima while it was under siege, until relief came on 20 April 1944. Not many of these left the battlefield unaided. My father,

Raymond Street, and some of the other survivors were kind enough to share their experiences with me. This is their story and is dedicated to those who did not return.

Robert Street
May 2013

Chapter 1

Early Days

I couldn't have been more than four or five. I was in a large room with a billiard table. We were at the house sale of some former high ranking military officer who had died. It was also a gunroom. My parents were there to see what they could buy for the second-hand furniture shop they ran. My father was going through my pockets taking away some live bullets that I'd got hold of and giving my mother a dressing down for not keeping an eye on me. I'd always had a fascination for guns and couldn't wait until I could buy my first air rifle.

We lived above a shop in Montpelier Villas, Cheltenham, later moving to the house at the rear. Early one morning, my mother woke me up. She said that we had to go and catch the train to Birmingham and that my father would follow later with the furniture. We were always moving around. My mother would set up in business, only to move on again when it failed or trade was so poor she couldn't go on. In Cheltenham trade was bad. It was time for a new start. We had relatives in Birmingham, so that was where we went.

In 1931 the country was still in the depths of the Depression. Being out of work was a way of life. My mother Ivy was the breadwinner, buying and selling second-hand furniture, paintings or whatever she could in her shop. She was a slim raven-haired woman with blue eyes, somewhat Jewish in appearance, which matched her business acumen. She married my father Arthur in 1917, shortly after he was invalided out of the First World War, wounded by a Turkish sniper's bullet. It ripped out most of his throat, damaging his vocal cords and leaving him with a hoarse, gravelly voice. He was a regular soldier, but had no trade or profession when he left the Army. He was only able to do casual work. Jobs were at a premium, so he was out of work most of the time. He had to sell his war medals and treasured collection of butterflies, caught during his days in India, to provide for us. His Army pension was only £1 per week. Mom earned what she could, but we never had enough.

In Birmingham Mom rented a shop in Hall Green, a somewhat posh area in the suburbs. My brother Eddie and I were sent to the local Hall Green School. Although my brother was able to settle down quickly, I found it difficult. Not only did I find the work hard, but I was left-handed and they made me use my right. The other children were quite snobbish and they taunted me because of my Gloucestershire accent, making me unhappy, so I played truant and was in trouble most of the time. My mother's new shop wasn't doing well so we moved to another part of town, Gladstone Road, Sparkbrook. I found myself at a new school, Golden Hillock Road. This was a working class, rough and ready sort of place, with teachers who could sort us out. I settled down well with these poorer children and started to enjoy school again. Despite the lack of wealth and their poor conditions, there was a general honesty about these inner city people. They would pull together in times of hardship. Doors were never locked, and we often walked freely to and from each other's houses without fear or worry. Of course, the immediate neighbours generally had several local relatives, so there was always a watchful eye to see that all was well. Our standard of living wasn't too bad, but we did have some hard times and often had to have Sunday dinner at one of our relatives' houses when money became short.

In the summer holidays I would go with Eddie to visit my Uncle George and our cousins. Uncle George was a builder. We would help make the concrete blocks for the new houses he was building. Each day we would travel a couple of miles to the building site in Wake Green Road, make blocks, riddle sand or undertake some other small task, all for a few sandwiches and three pence a day! It was worth it, we had the time of our lives.

The next few years were much the same: Mother opening and closing shops and us all moving from house to house in Birmingham. We eventually settled in Anderton Road. I was fourteen and had finished school. I worked in a local bakery, bringing home hard-earned cash, much needed for the family kitty. We stayed at Anderton Road for four years before moving around the corner into Palmerston Road. This was my mother's finest business venture. Somehow she managed to retain our old house in Anderton Road and took lodgers into both, my father collecting the rent and doing the odd jobs and repairs. She eventually acquired seven more houses for the same purpose. These were happy times for me.

However, things weren't all good; the Depression was still on, leaving many people poverty stricken. Most working class people weren't that well paid and lived on the breadline. This meant that if you were out of work for any amount of time it could have serious implications for family life. Poverty goes hand in hand with poor health, and diseases such as tuberculosis and rickets were rife. I caught scarlet fever and spent weeks isolated in an attic room, cut off from everybody except my mother and father. Even my brother wasn't allowed to see me. My father used to sit with me in the evening armed with a bottle of beer, light a cigarette and tell me about his days in the Army, until I fell asleep. I used to say, 'Tell me about India, Dad' or 'Tell me about the war, Dad'. Little did I think that in ten years' time I would go to those parts of India where he'd been.

He'd been a regular soldier since 1911, not one of those men suddenly swept away by the emotion of patriotism in 1914. He was part of the coronation parade for King George V before being sent to India to serve. In 1915 he was called into action to fight in the Dardanelles.

He told me of his battalion, the 4th Worcesters and their landing on W Beach at Gallipoli. They were following the 1st Lancashire Fusiliers, who had run into a strong contingent of Turkish troops defending positions on the cliffs above. They landed to be met by a hail of bullets cutting down the young soldiers in vast numbers. As the waves broke on the shore the sea was red with the blood of the dead and wounded. As they tried to move up the beach to the path to mount the cliff, my father spoke to a young officer from the Lancashires who looked like he was clinging to the cliff face, only to find that he was actually dead. They eventually got to the top, advanced several miles inland and dug in.

My father's job was to man a Vickers machine gun. As the darkness drew in, he set the gun to hit any attacking enemy in the lower part of the body or the legs. During the night noises were heard in no-man's-land. My father was ordered to fire into the darkness, and this was met immediately by the screams and moans of the enemy. In the light of the day, he witnessed large groups of dead and wounded Turks, many with limbs hanging off where the bullets from his machine gun had cut them down. He and his comrades did what they could for the wounded, putting their packs under their legs to support them, giving them water and tending their wounds as best they could. This was far better treatment than some of our boys got from the Turks, who apparently often tortured them to death and left them nailed to wooden crosses.

A couple of weeks later, my father was firing his Vickers at the Turkish front line, causing havoc in their enemy trenches. A sniper's bullet hit his machine gun's water cooling casing around the barrel, but he calmly plugged the bullet hole and opened fire again. Another bullet thudded into the path alongside him, but again he focused on his target, relentlessly sending a shower of machine gun bullets into the enemy position. Suddenly, a blow like a sledgehammer hit him across the throat, knocking him backwards. A sniper's bullet had ripped his throat open, severing his windpipe and causing him to start choking on his own blood. He couldn't cry out because his vocal cords had been damaged. His comrades roughly bandaged his wound and dragged him away from his machine gun to a safer place.

Left alone, he had the choice of staying there and bleeding to death or attempting to make his way to the first aid dressing station. Unaided, picking out bits of shattered bone-like tissue from his wound in order to breathe and feeling cold with shock and loss of blood, he unstrapped an unused greatcoat from a dead Turk, put it on and crawled back towards the dressing station. There he sat down on the ground, joining the many other waiting wounded. There was a constant barrage of shell fire exploding all around the area, and suddenly my father felt as if he was sitting in water. When he looked down, he saw a stream of blood flowing underneath him. The wounded man next to him had been killed, ripped apart by shrapnel, and his blood was now saturating the ground beneath.

By this time my father was very weak and heard that one of the officers was going round shooting badly wounded soldiers to put them out of their misery. Mercy killing, they called it. He didn't want that, so after a lull in the shellfire he moved to another dressing station further back and eventually arrived at a troop ship, the *River Clyde*, where he was operated on. He wasn't allowed any anaesthetic. They had to put in a plastic tube to reconnect his windpipe and he had to be awake so that they could be sure he could breathe. It worked, but was extremely painful, and the wound had to be left gaping to heal on its own. He was sent to a hospital in the Middle East for convalescence. That was the end of his war. At the age of twenty-four his Army career was over. He spent the rest of the war testing machine guns in England, later to be discharged with a War Pension of just £1 per week.

During my long illness with scarlet fever he would repeat these and other stories about his Army days as I drifted off into unconsciousness, waking up later eagerly asking for more. It was only much later, when in action myself, that the true horror and extent of his suffering became clear. Only then I could fully understand what he'd been through. However, not all his stories were of the bloodthirsty deeds of war. Many were vivid descriptions of his day-to-day life in exotic lands, where he painted in my mind colourful pictures of faraway countries and people, of tigers, elephants and other animals I'd only ever seen in picture books.

I still recall my excitement when he told me stories of how he caught exotic butterflies in pine forests with a simple net attached to a bamboo pole and how, whilst hunting these insects, he was stalked by a young tiger, noticing it peering at him from behind trees and undergrowth, but not attacking him. He believed it was probably put off by the long bamboo pole. In any event, my father calmly continued on his way and walked back towards his camp. These stories left me in awe, but although I didn't know it then, I too in the future, would visit such exotic places, treading in his footsteps.

My friends and I were too young to drive. The only alternative form of personal transport was a pushbike, but money was tight. We hadn't been working long and didn't have any spare cash. The answer was to build our own, so we did. We searched everywhere, scavenging scrap parts from the bottom of gardens, hedges, sheds and scrapyards. Our parents lent us the money to buy some new brakes, though. Then there we were, boasting a 'new' bike to go to work, fishing or camping. We would go away at weekends or holidays. Many a time, a crowd of us would get on our bikes and ride to Bidford-on-Avon or other local places, fishing, swimming, camping or simply taking in the countryside. Holidays were rare and had to be within pedalling distance.

My first 'real' full-time job was in a bakery, working in a cold basement preparing dough and putting it into silver foil trays for custard tarts and pork pies, then taking them upstairs to a hot uncomfortable bakery. I was earning twelve shillings a week, but worked long hours for it. I started at eight in the morning, finishing at six at night and at lunchtime on Saturdays. After that I went to work for a welder in Evelyn Road, but had to leave when I had scarlet fever. When I was better I got a job at Cashmores, a grocer's shop on the corner of Poplar Road and Stratford Road in Sparkhill. Again it was long hours, but the pay was better and I got some perks, such as free food. It was in the yard here, moving stock on a frosty morning, that I slipped and fell backwards on to a cast iron rainwater pipe. I was completely numb and couldn't move. I forced myself up and continued working, but the damage was done to my back. The doctor wanted me to wear a special back-brace, but I wouldn't. As it healed it became slightly twisted.

I spent the next few years going from job to job. All of the family were in work, and for the first time I had money to spend. I bought a 'Diana' air rifle. I'd always wanted one. It was twelve shillings and and sixpence (62½p), but I couldn't afford to pay for it outright, so I bought it 'on the weekly', a shilling or so per week. I couldn't take it away. The shopkeeper wouldn't let me have it until it was fully paid for. I had to use my old one in the meantime. After a few weeks, my mother gave me the money to pay it off. I think she felt sorry for me. The rifle gave me a lot of pleasure, and I would often play with it in the garden with my best mate, Sammy. He lived next door. We lined up old style 'gypsy' washing-line pegs and had competitions shooting at them. We became pretty good shots in the end, even shooting pennies out of each other's hands.

Things seemed to be on the up. I got my cousin Henry's old job at a firm of French polishers, working in a large workshop above some garages. Sammy worked there too. Here I learnt some of life's hard and fast rules. The friendly older staff would teach us the basics, such as sharing cigarettes, food, drink or whatever. If you had only two cigarettes left, you would share them with someone who had none, not hide them away. When you were broke, the favour would be returned. These were good times despite the hardship. We were growing up quickly and learning all the time. At lunchtimes we would play cards for cigarettes. It was horrible at first, as both Sammy and I soon owed over one hundred cigarettes to our fellow workers. I was worried sick, but not Sammy. He found a tobacconist that sold cheap Russian ones. They were half the price of the regular brands. They tasted vile, but we bet these instead of the more expensive English ones. We soon got the hang of things and paid off our debts using these cheap cigarettes, keeping the more pleasurable Park Drive or Woodbines for ourselves. Sammy moved on to work in a fish and chip shop, where it was better pay. Shortly after, his mum remarried and they moved away, after which we lost touch. He did come back later in 1937 and told us he'd joined up. He went to India and served in the Middle East during the war, but was captured and held as a prisoner of war. I saw him once more, in 1947, but later heard that he'd died in the late 1980s.

I had new friends now: my brother Eddie, cousin Henry and their mob. We made quite a crowd, dressed in our thirty-bob tailored suits, trilby hats, overcoats and leather gloves, imitating Humphrey Bogart, James Cagney and other macho film stars. The others were older and could drive. I couldn't and was envious when they took girls out for romantic drives in the country.

On 3 September 1939, we were listening to the radio and heard Neville Chamberlain announce war with Germany. The next few years were to drastically change all of our lives, but things continued as usual for a few months. I tried to join up straight away, but was told to come back when I was twenty-one.

In 1940 things accelerated somewhat. Eddie was called up, as were some of our cousins and friends. A few months later, things started to hit home: a friend was killed at Dunkirk and another taken prisoner.

We soon we realized that the war wasn't going well for us. There was a radio appeal for volunteers to protect our district from German paratroopers. They wanted men between the ages of sixteen and sixty-five. I joined immediately. While I was getting ready to leave there was a knock at the door. My mate Jackie Waring had had the same idea. I had known Jackie from my school days; he was one of the original lot that used to come on the cycling and fishing trips when we were kids. We enrolled at Sparkhill Police Station and were led through the back to a room to meet a crowd of men being shown how to use a rifle.

The next night we reported to Taunton Road Barracks, where we were put into patrols and given steel helmets and armbands with 'LDV' (Local Defence Volunteers) on them. We were handed a clip of five .303 bullets. They didn't give us a rifle to fire them, but they did give us a pickaxe handle for our first dusk to dawn patrol. It was on the playing fields near Moseley Grammar School. The tower of the school building was used as a lookout post to plot the position of fires after air raids. An ex-First World War NCO was in charge. We nicknamed him 'Old Bill', due to his similarity to a First World War cartoon character. He was clearly senior to us and a right character. He had an awful habit of hiding in hedges and bushes, then suddenly jumping out in the pitch blackness of the night shouting, 'Who goes there?' The panic-stricken people would give their identity whilst he held his bayonet inches from their throats. When satisfied, he would remove the bayonet saying, 'Pass, friend' in his strong Brummie accent, at the same time blowing his beery breath over them. He kept us on our toes and we would be extra vigilant if we knew Old Bill was on duty. He had the only rifle in the patrol, a .303 Lee Enfield. He told us that if he got killed or wounded, one of us should grab the rifle and continue the fight using our own clip of bullets. Until then the pickaxe handle was to be our only weapon of defence against any Nazi paratroopers.

We undertook our dawn to dusk patrols several nights each week, adding to our kit and uniform as more became available; the old Army greatcoats were much appreciated in the winter. Within a month we each had our own rifles and fifty rounds of ammunition. Bayonet and rifle practice followed. By the time I left to join up we had been properly armed, even having machine guns and grenades.

On one occasion, whilst patrolling during an air raid, we noticed a light flashing from a nearby tree. We guessed that it was an enemy agent. We quickly chased after him but some idiot shouted and gave the game away. He immediately jumped from the tree on to a motorbike and disappeared into the darkness. During another raid, someone in the tower saw a flare being launched from behind a big empty house, lighting up the sky. It was to guide the German bombers on to their targets. Our patrol rushed over to search the house, but couldn't find anyone there. Later, a strange character infiltrated our Home Guard. He was a thick-set, beer-swilling chap. He appeared rather suddenly on the scene, but had no real background. He was a young man of about twenty and well educated, but although I didn't notice it, there was a tell-tale sign in his accent that the ex-First World War soldiers thought they recognized as German. The police came and took him away.

The war effort was mobilizing quickly, but the horrors of war were soon apparent as the German bombers carried out their raids. The primary target was the BSA munitions factory in Small Heath, just around the corner from where we lived. Tyseley railway sidings, not far away, were also targeted to disrupt communications and freight. Our first experience of horror was during September and October 1940. We saw hundreds of lights in the distant skyline, the enemy aircraft having dropped flares to light up the city beneath. Bombs exploded and fires raged, shedding more light on the targets. We patrolled near Swanshurst Park, Moseley, where the anti-aircraft guns were stationed. These thundered a barrage of flak at the enemy aircraft as they approached, to try to prevent them reaching their targets. Huge red flashes high up in the sky chased the aircraft as they flew over. Suddenly, showers of hot metal fell from the sky, forcing us to shelter under hedges and trees. It turned out to be shrapnel from our own flak. Later we saw more of this in the streets around the town, but this time we were wearing our steel helmets.

It was different at home during the raids. Air raid shelters (Anderson shelters, as they were called) were provided. These were constructed of corrugated metal sheet on an angle iron frame. The council provided them. They didn't put them up, they were simply left outside people's houses for them to put together themselves. Everybody mucked in, helping the old or less fortunate. The idea was to position the shelter in the garden away from the house, with the base about four feet below ground, so that people could get underground during air raids. We had one in our garden, but it was too cold in the winter, so we stayed indoors sitting on the cellar steps. My father, on the other hand, wasn't too bothered about the raids at all and would often stay in the house or go out. On one occasion there was a near miss: a bomb had gone off about thirty yards away from our house. It blew the windows out and took the front door off its hinges. We couldn't find my father anywhere and were really worried. He eventually turned up with a bottle of beer as if nothing had happened. He'd been to the outdoor toilet. Relieved that he was safe, we carried on putting out the incendiary bombs in the garden and street and set about repairing the damage.

As the spring approached in 1941, the fear of invasion had passed and our guard duties were cut to two nights a week. I was twenty-one, working as a tool setter. This was a 'reserved occupation' and prevented me from being conscripted. I don't know why. All I did was put spanner blanks into a machine. It wasn't that clever. I felt it was time to join up, but failed the Army medical over slight deafness in one ear. I couldn't believe it. I was really disappointed to have to return to my boring job.

The Home Guard duties still continued and more training given. In October I arrived at Taunton Road Drill Hall one evening at about a quarter to eight. A doctor was to give a first aid lecture on how to help any wounded after an air raid. The Carlton Picture House was opposite. I almost decided to give the lecture a miss and see the film Typhoon as I had been waiting for this to come around for ages. Reluctantly, I put duty before pleasure and went into the Drill Hall and upstairs to the lecture room. I looked over towards the picture house foyer as the blackouts were drawn covering the windows. A single electric light bulb lit our room and about twenty of us took our seats as the doctor arrived and began. As he talked the sirens started to wail. An air raid was imminent. The doctor carried on talking, showing us how to dress wounds. The bombs were getting nearer. As things got worse he asked if we wished him to continue. Of course, we all agreed. No one wanted to show they were scared. Suddenly the blackouts were blown into the room, the light went out and the room rocked, filling up with dust and smoke. We were thrown to the floor by the blast. We looked with amazement through the shattered windows and the lights came on in the picture house opposite. Someone shouted to put the lights out and we all rushed downstairs in confusion. The picture house had received a direct hit. The bomb had gone off in front of the screen. The manager had put the lights on to help the wounded. When the raid had started earlier he had cleared the front rows of seats of all but a few people, moving most of them under the balcony, for apparent safety. Still a lot were killed or wounded. The lights were left on for a few minutes so the wounded could be taken from the wrecked cinema. The dead had to wait until after the raid finished.

The doctor organized us to tend to the wounded outside. An usherette had been blown on to the road and was moaning. The doctor ordered us to carry her over to the barracks on a door that was lying on the pavement by her. We walked round a large crater from a second bomb that had fallen in the middle of the road, right outside the window of the lecture room which we were in earlier.

When we finally entered the cinema, it was terrible. There was a crowd of wounded people, some sitting, others lying on the floor of the entrance. A badly wounded girl lay near the door crying for her mom. Someone started taking names and addresses so that families could be told. The doctor and others bandaged the wounded. A middle-aged man sat near the injured girl. He had a hole the size of a penny in his forehead but seemed all right, quite normal in speech and talking coherently and answering when others spoke to him.

With one of the NCOs we continued on out through the semi-dark foyer, to search the seats inside the picture house. It was wrecked, the seats all covered with dust and rubble everywhere. Most of the front part of the roof had been blown away, the night sky providing the only light to help us search.

Someone noticed a figure in the seats over the other side. The NCO shone a torch. It was a woman with her hands clasped together, sitting quite comfortably as one would do to watch the film. Closer inspection showed that the woman had no head, just a dusty blood-covered stump of a neck. It was horrific. We moved on. Near the front a young lad of about twelve was between the front seats. The NCO checked him but he was dead too, curled up as if asleep. Further round we found two more people, a man and a woman, clearly a bus driver and conductress. There were no marks on them. They were just in their seats as if asleep. They had also been killed by the blast. We searched the rubble a little more before leaving it for others to deal with. As we went back to the foyer, we found the man with the hole in his forehead had died, as had the young girl lying by the door. Others were also dying, some from shock, some from their injuries. It wasn't until one in the morning that several vans came to collect the dead and wounded.

When we left the building we were told to man the end of the road to prevent anyone coming through, with the exception of the emergency services. Four of us were detailed, two on the left hand side of road and two on the other corner. A thickset man tried to enter, but we halted him, telling him that the road was closed and we were ordered not to let anyone through. He became angry but soon shut up when he found two bayonets pushed hard against his throat. One of the older NCOs came across to calm the situation down, and the man left hurling rounds of abuse; but we'd seen enough for one night to put up with him.

We then returned to the barracks and were told to go to the canteen for a drink and some food, but I couldn't eat. That first horror of the war had taken my appetite away. Even the beer tasted flat.

It was four in the morning when we came off duty. We walked to my mate Jackie Waring's road, only to see that many of the buildings were on fire. It was a right mess. We ran to Jackie's house, but fortunately it was not damaged. After he checked to see his family were all right I made my way home to get some sleep in what was left of the night as I had to go to work. My parents were glad to see me. They'd heard about the bombing and were worried. The horror of that night stayed with me for ages. I couldn't eat for days.

The air raids continued, causing havoc and misery. Incendiary bombs would set buildings ablaze, lighting up the city skyline and guiding more bombers on to the area, whether it was a target that was actually pre-selected or not. One night the fires were so bad that I saw the brickwork on one building glowing red with the heat. The firefighters doused it with water and the colour changed to black, but it went red again as soon as the hose was moved away to another area. The firemen had an awful time. I don't know how they coped.

The days after the raids were spent trying to recover some semblance of order, but it was hard. I remember seeing a factory operating with a large area of the roof missing. A bomb had damaged it, blowing over a big machine press. Somehow the press was righted and business continued, despite the absence of the roof.

In December 1941 we heard that the Japanese had attacked Pearl Harbour. The Americans were now in the war on our side. I felt that I was only playing at soldiers in the Home Guard. With all the fears of invasion gone and the Americans on our side, I felt I wasn't doing enough. I'd had a protected occupation in various factories since 1938; when, for instance, I worked for a company called Ash and Lacey, the manager refused to release me for national service. Now, at my current job, every day dragged. I felt trapped. I just seemed to be clock-watching all day. Speakers blared out some of the current popular tunes to try to reduce the boredom, but I felt I had to get out before I went mad.

In March 1942 I took a Monday off and went down the Recruiting Office to try for the third time to join up. The recruiting sergeant told me I was in a reserved occupation and said what an important job I was doing to help the war effort. This didn't wash with me. I needed to join the Army to achieve something with my life. I said I was keen to join up because of my family history of regular soldiering. Eventually, he said if I was prepared to join the Army for seven years, with five years on reserve service, they would take me. I thought quickly and said, 'Yes'. I was then sent for a medical. When the medic got to the hearing test he whispered into my ear but I didn't hear anything. I gave the right answer, though, as I knew it from the previous times. I successfully asked to join my father's regiment, the 4th Battalion of the Worcestershire Regiment. The next day I told my mate Jackie and he followed suit, joining the same regiment.

Following in my father's footsteps, my training was to take place in the same old Victorian Norton Barracks, Worcester. I was to report on 16 April 1942. When I got home my parents went mad. Mom was in tears and Dad said I was a fool. However, they came round to it in the end.

Jackie and I gave notice, left our jobs and handed in our Home Guard uniforms. I was finally in the Army. I'd never been away from home for any real length of time before, certainly not any great distance, but here we were, going to be trained to fight in a war, perhaps half way round the world. Of course, I didn`t think of it like that. In fact, in the Army they didn`t give you time to think, they kept everyone busy. The NCOs (Non-commissioned officers) shouted and hurried us into the lorries waiting to take us to Norton Barracks. We threw our cases on, climbed aboard and away we went along country lanes. It was like going on holiday at first, but people were talking and laughing too much, some chain-smoking. We were thinking about what was to come next, especially those that had been called up (as opposed to the volunteers), perhaps leaving their wives and children. I had thoughts of whether I could cope and what would happen if I couldn`t. I quickly put these to the back of my mind.

We got off the lorries at the Barracks and stood in three lines next to our suitcases. The NCO pointed out some very smartly dressed soldiers performing drill, whilst their Drill Sergeant barked out orders at them. When he said he would make us better and smarter than them my heart sank. I felt that I'd made the biggest mistake of my life joining up for seven years. We handed over our suitcases, which were to be taken home on our first leave, swapped our civvy clothes for Army uniforms, collected our kit and were sent to our billets. Then it was off to the NAAFI for sandwiches and drinks. Our billets were in old Victorian blocks. We were allotted an area just big enough for an old fashioned, two-tier metal bunk bed and our kit. Every morning, blankets were to be folded at the foot of the bed and our packs neatly laid out. Time seemed to race as we did this, washed, shaved, polished our boots and cleaned our badges and buttons before parade. It was a shock to most of us. We weren't used to making beds and housework. We had the Army short-back-and-sides haircut, dentist's and medical inspections and numerous inoculations. A week of square bashing followed, and we were confined to barracks to get used to Army life. We weren't allowed out until they considered we looked and acted like proper soldiers. As the weeks passed we went through extensive training until we were at the peak of fitness and fully up to speed with Army disciplines.

Training was under a strict regime, supervised by NCOs in a no-nonsense manner. On parade the slightest misdemeanour would result in a charge. We started using live ammunition, and during grenade practice it was my turn to have a go. The target was a wooden stump some distance away. I'd never thrown a grenade before. When I did, it went up almost vertically, landing about ten yards in front of us. The NCO shouted, 'Down!' We all threw ourselves to the ground and lay flat with our faces in the mud. The grenade exploded, but no one was hurt. The NCO was not pleased.

We'd get a pass some weekends and return home. We'd slip a driver a shilling each for a lift in one of the Army lorries if we could. At home we'd visit family and friends and go to the Royal Oak pub, on the corner of Alfred Street and Stoney Lane. A friend of Jackie's dad ran it and organized a collection for locals who had joined up, keeping it in a large bottle on the bar. Each soldier could have ten shillings' worth of drinks from the kitty, so Jackie and I went to claim ours. We had a great time. When I got home, I could sense the worry that my mother had, but I was selfish. I didn't consider others and would joke about it. I didn't think I'd be killed or wounded. I just wanted to live life to the full. I accepted the Army even if I didn't really like it, but it was better than being trapped in a job I hated in war-torn Britain.

After we had done six weeks of training in July 1942 we had our passing out parade. We moved from Worcester to a camp at Market Rasen, Lincolnshire. This camp was different from Norton Barracks, the land being flat and surrounded by pine trees. Instead of Victorian-style barracks there were Nissen huts, large rectangular buildings with semi-circular corrugated metal roofs. They were freezing in winter and unbearably hot in summer. It was too far away for weekend leave in Birmingham. We had to make do with the local nightlife or a weekend in Grimsby, the nearest big town.

We seemed to be undertaking endless route marches. We marched 30 miles a day with a full pack and weapons, and the same the next day. It was a hell of a sight: neat lines of soldiers as far as you could see, marching through lovely unspoilt countryside. This was strange to us as we were used to the city, but here we were in the country, marching down beautiful lanes with fruit-laden trees and wild raspberries.

Once we marched to Scarborough, over 100 miles with a full pack. A thousand men took part, marching 30 miles each day with only ten minutes' rest every hour. We had to take turns to carry heavy weapons such as the Bren gun which made it worse. I prayed I'd get my turn early on in the march, as I couldn't imagine being able to carry it later. At the end of the day we would we would set up camp at a nearby farm and nurse our blisters, tired feet and legs. Meals were prepared in a field kitchen and toilets dug in a field close by. I was physically sick at the end of each day with exhaustion and would rush to the toilets, where I'd have to squat precariously over two horizontal wooden poles, taking care not to fall into the stinking mess below. The camps were usually in the middle of nowhere, and we roughed it, sleeping on straw or hay in some old barn or outbuilding, making the best of it and getting what sleep we could before the next day. As if 30 miles' marching wasn't enough, some of the men would ask where the nearest pub was and walk three miles or so for a drink, then walk back again. They must have been mad. I didn't bother. I got as much rest as I could. Near the end of the march we took one of our rest breaks by a bus stop. We were well tired. A bus turned up and a lady took pity on us. She had a quick chat and threw down three packets of cigarettes for us to share. We crossed the River Humber on a ferry called the *New Holland* and marched to the next camp. As we approached, relieved and looking forward to completing the march, the commanding officer's jeep stopped and he ordered us to run the last 200 yards. It was torture.

After a rest we then went on to the moors to do some weapon training, before finally returning to our Market Rasen camp. It was then that we found the Army allowed a small percentage of casualties during training. We were put under mortar attack to train us to cope with the pressure and stress of an enemy barrage. Others were training to aim the mortars. Their aim wasn't any good and the mortar bombs dropped too close, getting closer as the barrage went on. An NCO who had to stand up and signal to the mortar group that they were dropping short was lucky when one dropped right by him, a piece of shrapnel only slicing off the end of his nose.

One of our chaps at Market Rasen was called Barton. He was always in trouble, but was a great sportsman. The Sergeant Major liked him and wanted him to remain on the camp staff to play for the football team, but Barton wanted to be drafted with his mates. The Sergeant Major said that if he stayed he would be promoted to an NCO and not go to war. Barton wouldn't have any of it. As our lorry moved off, Barton was last on board. The Sergeant Major stood in the middle of the road shouting, 'I shall be saluting your memorial, you silly bastard.' Barton swore quietly as he got on. (The Sergeant Major was right. Barton was killed in action two years later).

Chapter 2

India: Bombay, Raniket and Lucknow

In December 1942 we found our names on a draft list. We went to Purley, where we were put up in newly built detached houses, all with modern bathrooms and inside toilets. Many of us were not used to such grandeur. Every room was filled to capacity. We were each allocated an area of bare floorboards to set out our bedding with our kit on top. After a few days we were all issued with tropical kit of sun helmets and shorts and then made to parade in the cold December weather, before being given two weeks' embarkation leave. This went by quickly, but I returned to my unit only to find that the draft had fallen through and we were given a further ten days' leave. I returned home for Christmas. In the New Year we were packed on to a troop train to Liverpool. It was for real this time.

It was 14 January 1943. We boarded an old liner called *Mooltan*. The ship was packed solid. We carried everything we had aboard and settled below in a small area on one of the decks with about fifteen others. A long wooden table was provided for meals. At one end was a porthole and above us hooks and beams to sling our hammocks. This was where we slept, ate meals and cleaned kit. Our hammocks were rolled up during the day and stowed at one end. We learnt the ship's drills and spent the day doing regular duties, but rested in the evening, playing cards, reading or discussing our unknown destination. The decks were highly polished wood and the Captain ordered us to be issued with plimsolls to prevent our boots damaging his beautiful decks. The ship was well armed with two six-inch guns at the stern and small guns mounted on the sides and top. We didn't worry about U-boats. We were confident that the Navy would look after us.

On our first morning, we woke to the noise of the ship's engines. We joined the main convoy at Greenock. We were told to carry life jackets at all times, these becoming our pillows at night. We were also given canvas bags with a small tin inside containing an emergency ration of chocolate. This was tied to our packs by a short piece of string. Many of us had our rations stolen by others cutting the string. I don't know why they bothered; the rations were horrible.

To keep the men occupied the NCOs arranged for a boxing ring to be erected below deck, and we were ordered to box three rounds with a chosen opponent. I was ordered to go up against a heavyweight, who had the reputation of being a hard man. I didn't have any choice. He obviously thought that I would be easy meat, but didn't realize that I had done boxing training before the war. Grinning all over his face, he ran at me like a bull at a gate only to meet my extended fist. I knocked him down and a big cheer went up from my mates. I was chuffed, but he got up. Less foolhardy now, he gave more thought to the fight, but I survived the three rounds to win on points. He wasn't happy and threatened to get his own back, but fortunately, he was later drafted elsewhere.

In February 1943 we arrived at Bombay. It smelt foul and the heat was almost unbearable. We had a few hours to look round. I'd never seen anything like it. There were snake charmers, beggars, knife throwers and street magicians who crowded round us hoping to get a few coppers. It was difficult to take it all in. The pavements seemed to be stained with blood, but we discovered that it was the residue of betel nuts, which the Indians chewed and spat out. There was poverty and squalor everywhere. Street traders, pimps and all sorts pestered us. Although my father had described the country in detail, nothing could have prepared me for the sights and sounds of India. It was a relief to leave Bombay and board a train to Allahabad Barracks.

The old steam train on which we were to travel was not an English-style Pullman as we expected, but more like those seen in Wild West films, with steps up to the back of the carriages and even an American-style cow catcher on the front of the engine. The carriages were split into compartments to hold six men, three on each side. That was where we slept or sat during the journey. Some of the other carriages had open areas to eat meals or drink tea made by those on cookhouse duty. One of us would go up to the driver of the train when it stopped and get hot water from the engine's boiler. We'd fill our bucket and add tea. Someone else would jab a couple of holes in a tin of Carnation Milk with his bayonet and throw in a handful of sugar, stirring it with the bayonet, and the bucket of tea would then be passed around. There were fruit- and *char-wallahs* at the stations. They sold fruit and tea in clay cups, working up to twenty-four hours a day for a pittance. We had Anglo-Indians with us who would help us haggle and agree a price.

We stopped at various stations, which were a fantastic sight, full of all sorts of people. The train never arrived or left on time, and local people must have been waiting ages for our train to turn up. When one was due, the station guard would strike a piece of old railway track that was hanging by a rope from one of the wooden beams of the station building. Hordes of people would appear from everywhere. It was like a scene from the Bible as they swept towards the train, dressed in their white flowing garments. All hell was let loose when they tried to get on. We were all right. We were in the part of the train reserved for British troops. The locals would run up to the train and throw their luggage on, only to see it thrown off by somebody else; but they all seemed to get on, hanging on to the sides, the roof or anywhere they could grab.

We stored our rifles under long wooden seats that lifted up. We would sit or sleep on top so no one could steal the guns. We had heard that Lee Enfield British rifles could be sold for up to one hundred pounds on the North-West frontier. Not only were we sleeping or sitting on top of our weapons, but all the doors were guarded by armed soldiers twenty-four hours a day and especially when the train stopped. As we travelled across the open country it appeared as if we were going back in time. The culture and the buildings were completely different to anything we'd seen before. This feeling increased when we stopped at an isolated station and an armed Indian Police escort led out a line of chained *dacoits* (armed robbers), wild looking men, to get aboard our train.

We eventually arrived at Allahabad to find the barracks, which consisted of modern brick-built blocks, together with sports fields, plunge baths and all mod cons. Native servants, or *dhobis* as they were called, were provided to keep us clean and smart, and they would lay our uniforms on our beds and attend to all our laundry and domestic needs. A servant arrived at five o'clock in the morning and shaved us each in turn while we were still half asleep under our mosquito nets in the long barrack room. We slept on *charpoys*, Indian-style bedsteads with woven rope in place of springs and three coconut fibre cushions instead of a mattress. Four bamboo poles supported our mosquito nets. At the foot of the bed our kit boxes were padlocked and screwed to the floor. The rifle racks were in the centre of the room, the weapons secured with a long, flat steel bar, chained and padlocked to prevent theft. An indoor plunge/swimming pool was provided and a night-time canteen. We had a compulsory 'bed down' after our midday meal, sleeping between two and four every day, the hottest hours, after which we would have tea at around five or six in the evening. After that, we would have some compulsory sports and then the remaining time was our own, unless we were detailed to battalion guard or picket duties. At night, in spite of fans, the temperature was still very high and the air was hot. You soaked the sheets with sweat and after getting up in the morning left a wet imprint of yourself on the bedding. It didn't matter, though, as the *dhobi* would change it.

It all seemed ideal, safe, sound and healthy, but it wasn't. The weather got hotter and hotter and the monsoon rains were imminent. The heat was almost beyond belief. It was so intense that on one occasion a man on parade broke rank, walked in a tight circle and fell on the ground with heatstroke. As the months went by, it got even hotter. Many of the beds in our barrack room became empty and were put up against the wall, their occupants being in hospital with heatstroke or one of the tropical diseases such as malaria or dysentery. This affected nearly 20 per cent of the men.

The authorities decided that the battalion was to be given ten days in the cool clean air of a mountain hill station in the Himalayas called Raniket. Although many of us had escaped the diseases associated with the heat of Allahabad, most of us suffered some sort of climate-change sickness due to coming from the hot, sticky atmosphere of

Allahabad to the cooler, thinner air of the mountains. We were warned to stay in twos whilst walking along the mountain roads with vegetation hanging over the sides, as men had been attacked by panthers and jackals. Guard duty was also done in twos but without a gun, just pickaxe handles. The rifles were locked away.

On one occasion I was woken for my stint on guard duty. I picked up my pickaxe handle. I was tired and half asleep. I saw a group of jackals rummaging around the dustbin area of the cookhouse but they immediately disappeared, as if melting into the darkness. I wasn't sure whether or not they had been there at all, but they had been, and they'd left for a reason. I saw a black head moving slowly from behind a grassy mound. It was a panther. That properly woke me up. I moved very quickly backwards into the hut, shut the door and raised the alarm. Several soldiers then cornered the animal on the rocky slope up the ridge behind the huts. I joined them to see what was going on. The panther started to come up the slope towards us, but soon changed his mind when he was showered with a hail of rocks and stones. He moved away quickly, and although I felt sorry for him, I reminded myself to keep my wits about me in the future. I could have easily have been his next meal. These were not the only creatures to be aware of. Many a time, a soldier would be walking back to his hut with a plate full of food, only to have a hawk swoop down and smash into the steel plate to steal the meat, leaving the rest spread on the ground.

We did jungle training in the foothills of the Himalayas. It was torturous in the heat and thin air. My pack straps cut into my shoulders and its weight seemed to increase by the hour. In the oppressive heat of one late afternoon we were marching along a mountain track bordering a deep ravine with a rock-strewn river below. Apart from short ten-minute breaks we had been marching for most of the day. We were expecting a surprise attack by a platoon of our own chaps. It was only training, but they would be using live ammunition. They told us not to worry as they wouldn't be aiming at us, but we weren't convinced. We started to move downhill, the trail widening and bringing us right down to a rocky ford across the river. On the other side there was a huge square rock, as big as a house, and we made our way across the river towards it. We were about half way across when the ambush started. The 'enemy' opened up with Bren guns and rifles, the bullets churning up the water around us and whining around the rocks. Their officer fired by our feet with his .38 calibre pistol as we rushed for the cover of the far river bank and large rocks. We fired back with our blank cartridges as we ran. Suddenly the distinctive noise of a live round was heard coming from our ranks and narrowly missing the officer. He wasn't pleased. He severely criticized our performance under the practice battle conditions but didn't pursue the question of how the live round came to be fired. We never knew who it was or whether it was intentional.

When I told people back home about the training they were amazed. They said we should have 'fallen out'. You couldn't. You wouldn't have had a chance out there alone. It was freezing at night and a rifle that only fired blanks in an area full of tigers, panthers and all sorts of snakes wasn't any good. You couldn't see anything on the dangerous mountain tracks. A leg or arm could easily be broken if you fell. One chap did fall out and spent a night alone on a rock. They found him the next day. He was in a right state and had to go to hospital. He never came back. I didn't fall out. I kept going. I'd sing a song to myself, think of what I'd do when I got back or even about the hot meal in the cookhouse at the end of the day; anything to take my mind off the task in hand.

While we were at Raniket Jackie and I volunteered for a three-day trek around a location called Almora. My father had visited there many years earlier and often spoke about it. Everyone else thought we were mad. They had done enough marching to last a lifetime and stayed in camp. We went anyway, about thirty of us, following our officer and an Indian guide on to a hillside jungle trail; our packs were stuffed with extra food, and their weight and the heat made us sweat. We lived rough and slept out on the slopes of the Himalayas, exploring the mountains and their streams and admiring the beautiful scenery. Overlooking and following a mountain stream we saw a water buffalo standing in the water drinking. Large trout-like fish fed in the cloudy water about his feet. It was a wonderful sight. The clear blue skies of the days brought bitter cold nights, which made sleeping difficult. We would level a space on the ground for our bedrolls and put ourselves in the most comfortable position to keep warm, looking forward to a welcome hot cup of tea in the morning. I remember watching the wind forming snow clouds on the mountain peaks as I drifted off to sleep. We arrived at Almora, but were not allowed into the town. As I looked from the mountainside it was just as I'd pictured it and I wondered what had changed since my father was stationed there all those years before. As we made our way back we noticed some small semi-circular stone structures called 'Dutch ovens'. My father spoke of these and of his unit marching through this area. They didn't have the luxury of lorries in those days and had to march and camp more often. Therefore, these Dutch ovens were built at particular points where a camp would be struck, to allow the cooks to prepare meals.

I was ordered to join the Garrison Police Force at Lucknow with a small Cockney chap. Our job was to police the area of the back-street brothels, arresting anyone going out of bounds, improperly dressed or causing trouble. It was a difficult job. We didn't want to be in the police force and were both too small to deal with any trouble. We had a little Gurkha officer in charge who was not impressed. He took us to a nightclub and told us to go in at ten o'clock and arrest anyone who was drunk or causing a disturbance. Well, this was a drinking haunt of the Irish Fusiliers, who were having a good time in the company of local girls. If they weren't drunk it would only be a matter of time before they were. We decided we wouldn't hang around and made our way out just before ten. We'd only just crossed the road when we heard screams, shouting and breaking glass.

Our invented excuse the next day was that we were chasing some soldiers who were out of bounds but that they had got away. The Gurkha officer didn't believe us. He warned us that if we didn't charge someone soon we would be sent back. The next night we charged two soldiers with being out of bounds. They stood calmly with their hands behind their backs. When we'd finished they moved forward, showing the rank insignias on their forearms. They were sergeant majors and immediately told us we hadn't charged them properly, so they charged us in turn. Fortunately, our Commanding Officer traded our charges off against theirs, but we lost our easy job in the Garrison Police.

On one occasion I met a beautiful Anglo-Indian girl who was seeing her relatives off. It was eleven o'clock at night and we chatted. She was white with jet black hair and had a Welsh accent. She came from a rich family and was taking a *tonga* (a small two-seater horse-drawn cab) back to her hotel. I felt at midnight this was unsafe, obtained permission from the NCO to let her ride in our Army truck and was pleased when she agreed. I enjoyed being close to this beautiful girl as the bumps in the road shook us together, and all too soon we halted outside her hotel. 'Don't be too long, Streety', said the NCO as I escorted her inside. A few minutes later a young dark-skinned man arrived at the hotel. She introduced him as her brother. I was shocked. I wasn't used to mixed families and found it hard to understand how she could be so white and he so dark. We chatted for a couple of minutes, then said our goodnights and I returned to the lorry and we headed back to our billet.

Our peacetime soldiering was now approaching an end and the monsoon was on its way. The heat was so intense that virtually all the vegetation had died, even the weeds. Everywhere was barren. A dead horse was found near the barracks. The poor thing had starved and vultures hovered around its corpse. They'd swoop down a short distance from the animal and then approach it with their characteristic stoop, shoulders hunched up. They looked like little old men as they walked. On reaching the animal they would tear away at its flesh.

At some point the monsoon broke and rain started to pour down at about two o'clock in the morning. We leapt out of our beds naked, dozens of us cheering and shouting. We stood outside letting the rain wash all over us, cooling down our bodies. Most of us had the red, itchy, prickly heat rash on us from sweating so much. Within days, grass and plants grew from the hard ground around the barracks. Leaves and blossom appeared on the trees as the waves of monsoon rain swept over us. Relief at last.

Chapter 3

The Arakan Campaign

It was October 1943 when we sent our Christmas cards home. They had to go then to be on time for Christmas. We were in the Arakan, a coastal area of western Burma near the Bay of Bengal. I couldn't believe it: Christmas in the paddy fields. The Japanese had advanced through Burma, pushing our troops back towards the sea. After travelling to Calcutta we sailed across the Bay to the rice port of Cox's Bazar, where we disembarked and waited to board the trucks that would take us through miles of paddy fields and scrubland. We were put on parade and told where we were going. I was standing next to my Brummie friend Jackie when the CO (Commanding Officer) brought his arm down in between us, declaring that those on my side would go with the Royal West Kents and those on Jackie's were to go with the 'Worcesters'. So that was that, we were to be split up. I was now in the 4th Battalion, the Queen's Own Royal West Kent Regiment, which formed part of the 161st Indian Infantry Brigade in the 5th Indian Division (later the Fourteenth Army). It was December 1943, and the Royal West Kents had already arrived from the Middle East.

The Arakan, a land of paddy fields and dense jungle-covered foothills, was to be our home for the next few months. Small streams or virtually dried-up rivers called *chaungs* ran through this countryside, providing water for the paddies. The forested foothills stood out like small islands in a sea of rice, and each hill was its own kingdom of jungle and wildlife. Across the Arakan lay our objective, the Tunnels. These ran through a backbone of mountains called the Mayu Range and had been built for a railway which was never completed. Our role was to push across the Arakan and clear the Japs from their positions in the foothills.

We waited for the lorries so we could move forward. Dozens of native workers threw basins of water from shallow holes dug at the side of the paddy fields on to the hot, dusty road. This was done to keep the dust from rising as the lorries passed which might be seen by aircraft or Jap scouts. Despite their efforts the dust rose everywhere, but fortunately no attack took place.

By early December 1943, almost a year since we had set sail from Liverpool, my war was about to begin for real. The days now passed quickly as our jungle training took place, marching through knee-high grass trying not to make any noise. We were told to watch out for leeches attached to the waving grass. (One sergeant died when he fell asleep by a stream; he got covered in leeches and lost too much blood). We had to make sure anything that rattled was secured, especially during night marches. This was my first Christmas away from home, and I can still remember eating a Christmas dinner of roast duck and vegetables, washed down with a bottle of beer, whilst sitting on a *bund* earth wall (embankment) by a paddy field. We were lucky. The men at the front line only had bully-beef and biscuits.

I had a feeling of wonder about this whole new world. I didn't think too much about the Japs. It never occurred to me that I might be killed. That always happened to the other guy. We were still very 'green'. We had never faced the enemy. One night as we moved towards a forward position and prepared to camp, the NCO told us to scrape an area of ground to prepare it for our groundsheets. I was getting ready when he noticed I had a white sheet in my pack. He told me to bury it. It would be no use in the front line. We were ordered to take supplies of bully-beef to our company, positioned on a nearby foothill, but a sniper was shooting at anyone who tried to get through. Our officer had a brainwave: he suggested we pile several large tins of this bully-beef on a stretcher, cover it with a blanket and take it to the hill. He reckoned the sniper wouldn't shoot stretcher-bearers. We loaded up the stretcher, and the officer told us to go. Part way across, someone slipped and we dropped the cans of bully-beef into the flooded paddy field. The officer shouted for us to pick up what we could and run back. I was in a mess; I hadn't had time to do up my belt in the initial rush to leave, and as I grabbed a tin my trousers started to come down. Nevertheless, I wasn't going to stand on ceremony. I rushed back as quickly as possible, trousers at half-mast. We were lucky the sniper didn't fire. The officer then told us to run across with a tin each, and we did, but my heart was in my mouth the whole time. I think the sniper had gone, but we weren't to know that.

The night was pitch black when we made our first infiltration through the Jap lines to take over some foothills behind them. After several miles of marching we reached our first foothill without trouble and dug in. By daylight a Jap sniper had found us and he was firing from the hilltop at people's heads. We dug a long crawl-trail trench about two feet deep so that with our heads below the bushes we were lower down and out of sight of the sniper. We were learning quickly, but they knew we were there. There were no refunds or second chances now. I was scared, but you had to keep it under control. It was a rotten feeling, creeping through the undergrowth knowing a Jap sniper could take a pot shot at you at any moment.

The next day, Bren gun carriers rolled up with our supplies, and a party of men were picked to go down and unload them. A young chap near me was picked and he went to the Bren carriers and started to unload, directed by Company Sergeant Major Gammon. Five minutes later, a barrage of 75mm Japanese shells blasted both the men and the Bren carriers. Three people were killed, including Sergeant Major Gammon; a shell landing by him ripped off his face. Another soldier gave a look of shock and horror as a piece of shrapnel smashed into his chest and he dropped to the ground dead. The Bren carriers moved out quickly. None were destroyed, but the unloading party had been knocked about. We were shocked by the sudden barrage. The young chap who had been with me survived with minor cuts and scratches to his ankle. He wasn't bothered but got one of the Medical Officers to dress it and limped off to his trench. Later, his leg became infected and he had to be taken back to hospital and out of the action. The Bren carriers came again the next day, and this time I was detailed to be one of the unloading party. I dreaded leaving my position. A barrage of shells came over but fortunately they were wide of the mark and no one was hurt. This time our own artillery replied, and we heard shells burn and buzz through the air and land with the thuds of explosion on the Japanese positions.

Our infiltrations continued, and we eventually encircled the Japanese and captured the rice port of Maungdaw on the Naff River in early January 1944. It was said to be an important port, but it looked to me like a couple of tin shacks and a jetty. We stayed there one night but we didn't get much sleep. We were camped near some trees with a type of large grapefruit on them. These kept falling to the ground during the night with loud thuds, and this kept us awake.

Paddy fields were everywhere, but they were dry and empty at that time. Whether it was because of the fighting or because the rice wouldn't grow, I didn't know, but there wasn't any cover. You tried to avoid crossing them if you could, but often you didn't have the choice. You soon learnt the tell-tale signs of danger, like patches of earth pock-marked by bullets. It was a relief to reach the other side of a paddy, where the rice and scrub offered some protection. I preferred to travel along the *chaungs*. These were often lined with banana bushes and gave excellent cover. One day I was crossing a *chaung* and noticed I was walking in someone else's footprints and that that someone was a Jap. They wore split-toed sandals so there was no mistaking those footsteps. They were only just filling with water so he could only be a minute or two in front of me. His footsteps went one way so I went the other.

The Royal West Kents had four rifle companies, A, B, C, D, and HQ Company. HQ supported these and Battalion Headquarters (BHQ), and the Commanding Officer (CO) was at BHQ. So was the Signals Officer (Captain John Topham), the Adjutant, the Intelligence Officer (Brian Dungay), the Medical Officer, signalmen and runners. I was the C Company Runner, attached to BHQ. Lieutenant Colonel John Laverty was in charge of the battalion. He was from Northern Ireland, but only had a slight accent. Major Peter Franklin was second in command. He was only about twenty-seven, but never seemed bothered by the responsibility. Major Short was the Adjutant. He was always smoking, Churchman No 1 being his brand of choice.

I preferred being a runner as I was happier on my own and felt safer that way. I took messages and laid and repaired lines of communication, sometimes cutting those of the enemy. I carried a little book that the officers had to sign each time I brought a message, so there was no way for me to shirk my job. I'd never have got away with it.

We were detailed to roll out a telephone wire to a foothill in front of us. It was at the end of a banana grove that was growing out of the water at the edge of a jungle river bed that led to the foothill. The wire was to be laid through the leaves above, which grew in such a way that they formed a tunnel over our heads. Our group of men moved slowly, ankle-deep in water. We expected a sudden burst of machine gun fire or the crump of Jap grenades, but it didn't come. We stood quietly in the water and the darkness, listening as the forward platoon of C Company moved on to the foothill without a shot being fired. A few minutes later, we advanced to take up our positions with the rest of them. After the signals had made contact with the new telephone wire we'd laid, I returned to BHQ with one or two others to stand by for more running duties. The next few days would see me returning once or twice a day with messages to this position. In the days that followed, Jap snipers moved in, looking, as likely as not, to pick off a runner and perhaps gain some information from the messages he carried.

I went out in the early hours of one morning with some medical orderlies (MOs). We were detailed to collect two bodies from the top of a deserted hill. These men had walked a few yards down a track and into the path of a sniper's fixed-line machine gun on the hill opposite. Somebody had put towels over their faces to prevent the flies getting to them. I could see that one was a sandy-haired NCO and I recognized him as one of those who had helped to sort us out into companies when we first arrived with the Royal West Kents several weeks before. The other was an Indian soldier. Both looked as if they were asleep, but they had been hit across the chest by a line of bullets. We eventually got them to the bottom of the hill, and they were buried as we stood guard, taking the map reference for the War Commission to identify their graves should they later want to recover the bodies (although I didn't give them much chance of doing so in this inhospitable terrain). But at least they were buried, which was more than can be said for many others.

As we waited for the men to finish we noticed another group of soldiers in the early morning mist on the paddy fields. Standing with our rifles ready to fire, we then recognized their jungle-green uniforms. They were one of our own guerrilla patrols. They had balaclava hats and blackened faces and most had Thompson machine guns without butts; they were geared up for close-quarter work behind the Jap lines. We'd been asked to volunteer as guerrillas soon after we landed in the Arakan, but I didn't fancy it. I was glad I hadn't volunteered when I found out what they had to do. After a brief chat and a smoke, which was fortunately hidden by the mist, they went on their way, and shortly after, with our job done, so did we.

I was relieved from my duties for a couple of weeks and someone took my place as BHQ runner. I was detailed to a trench that was the target of a Japanese fixed machine gun. The first day I arrived, one of the chaps there told me what was happening and said that I could dig the trench a little deeper if I liked. When I got in I threw a few shovelfuls of earth out to tidy it up, so to speak, and settled down. When the first sniping took place I thought I'd had it. The enemy machine gun relentlessly panned the parapet of my trench, the bullets zipping into the soil inches above me. I was sure they would come through the parapet and get me. After the firing finished I dug down a lot further, to about four feet. When the NCO came round he wasn't too happy and ordered me to get an ammunition box or something to stand on because the trench was too deep; he said that we were here to fight the enemy not hide from them. I thought to myself, it was all right for him to say that, he wasn't in there when the bullets were flying. I was warned by some of the others not to look over the parapet in the daytime and only take a quick look at night, as the sniper would fire intermittently. They were right. Every now and then my sniper would let off a short burst in the hope of catching me off guard. It was a nerve-racking time, but after a day or so I got used to it. A crawl-trench intersected with mine, and I was able to move out via this trench for meals. I would also nip into the next trench, which was safe, and spy through a hole in the forward wall to look for the sniper's position.

Sometimes those in the neighbouring trenches would ask me to throw up an empty cigarette packet to see in they could spot the sniper. I did, and each time it drew a burst of machine gun fire from the Jap. I continually teased the machine gunner into wasting his ammunition by throwing a handful of earth or a piece of stick out of the trench. During that two-week stint he must have wasted hundreds of rounds of ammunition.

Having to keep low down in the trench all day was boring, and I would spend my time carving out holes in the trench walls to form little shelves and alcoves for personal comforts such as a tin of jam or bully beef. Food was in short supply and I had to ration myself to just one spoonful of jam a day to make it last. The rest of the time I would spend writing letters or reading. Now and then the guys in the next trench would invite me to look through their field glasses to see if I could spot the sniper or any wildlife. I remember seeing a tiger eating a dead mule in a distant paddy field, but I never did see the sniper.

Many a time the Signals Officer, John Topham, would shout for the C Company runner, and my heart would sink. One such time, I had just finished my breakfast of baked beans and tinned soya mince sausages, washed down with a mug of tea. Still tired from lack of sleep after weeks of two hours on and two hours off night guard duty, I had hoped to rest a little after breakfast. Instead, I now had to push out into the paddy fields and an uncertain future. I grabbed my rifle and bandolier of fifty rounds of ammunition, took the message from the officer and started moving down the track off the hill to the paddy fields, passing bunkers and trenches on my way. Someone shouted, 'All right, Streety' to give moral support. I gave a grin and a wink to hide the fear I felt inside, replied, 'All right' and moved towards the jungle cover. It was late January 1944, and as I moved through the rice fields I saw mudfish, only a few inches long, basking on the banks. They rushed back into the water as I approached. Flocks of green and grey parrots flew overhead. They landed on a dead tree, seemingly bringing it back to life with their colourful plumage. I continued towards the distant foothill with my message.

One Jap patrol blundered on to a foothill held by the battalion and got wiped out. It was dark and they had been challenged by someone in the forward trench, but instead of retreating, the Japs kept coming, led by a huge NCO wielding a shovel and clearing a path up the jungle-covered hillside as he went. Most of them were killed outright, but he kept coming in spite of heavy fire. Nothing seemed to stop him. Suddenly a grenade exploded on his chest, taking part of his head off. Soon all was quiet again. I arrived on the hill the next day with a message from BHQ. They had buried the Japanese dead, but there was a smell of dried blood and death in the air. I delivered my message and stayed for a short while to look round.

It was the first time I'd seen Japanese weapons. They had a type of Bren gun which was much lighter than ours and fired a smaller bullet. Their rifles were longer, with a French-style bayonet, and fired the same small bullets. They had oblong leather ammo pouches, grenades, helmets and water bottles. I noticed a type of short-handled shovel or pointed spade for digging trenches and foxholes. I made a mental note to get hold of one of these shovels as soon as possible; they seemed better than ours. I did get one some weeks later, only to lose it after a few days.

Shortly after, we infiltrated at night through the Japanese lines and past enemy-held positions. Luckily for us, the paddy fields were covered in mist and we passed through unseen to take up positions behind the Japs, cutting their supply lines. The Japs soon found us and shelled and sniped our position, killing and wounding a number of our men. They were not happy to find us behind them and even more so when our artillery, air strikes and dive-bombers turned their positions from green to brown, blasting all the jungle cover away and causing landslides. Their foothill was lost to sight in the clouds of dust and smoke as barrage after barrage of shells smashed into their positions. Even so, after all this, they would open up with light machine gun fire to let us know they were still around. After one such attack, they retreated at night, using the mist just as we had done and leaving a few diehard soldiers behind to slow us up. Soon after, our patrols reported that there were no Japs for ten miles or so and we advanced to our next position.

We had to be alert at all times and took it in turns to sleep, two hours on, two hours off. It was a little easier to move at night but you had to let others know you were moving. We were all tense. They were a great bunch of chaps. We had a lot of Cockneys with us and they were always joking. Two of them were great pals. One of them went off to the toilet one night and didn't tell his mate, Larry, he was going. Larry later heard a movement behind him and fired – he had shot his pal. When he realized what he'd done, he flipped. He should have been sent back really, but there was no way they could do that. He surrounded his trench with bushes so no one could get in or out and shot at anything that moved. I was ordered to tell him to stand to one day, but I couldn't get through the bushes. I didn't try too hard, for fear he might open fire. I told the NCO and he decided to go himself. As he went up the hill we all watched and waited to see what would happen. There was a lot of wild shooting, but after a while the NCO came back and Larry stayed hidden in his trench.

Being a runner, I spent a lot of my time in no-man's-land or behind the enemy lines and had to learn very quickly about jungle warfare as the Japanese were more than experts in this field. I had to keep my wits about me all the time as the thick jungle vegetation of scrub bushes, trees and grasses, sometimes six feet high or more, not only provided good cover for myself, but also for the Japs. A sniper could burrow through a small entrance at the base of these high weeds, and once inside could hollow out an area into a small room. He could then wait patiently to strike, even sleeping in there.

It was around this time we heard that the Japs had surrounded the 7th Indian Division in the pass on the other side of the Mayu Range of mountains to our rear. We were told that they had broken through and swept down the mountain road, overrunning a hospital, bayoneting wounded soldiers in their beds and chopping off the doctors' hands to prevent them treating anybody. Our troops were cut off but had formed a box-like defence, from where they fought off Japanese attacks and stayed put until the numerically weaker enemy withdrew. Others cleared the area of enemy troops and repaired communications. We now had to withdraw from the hill we held and move to fresh company positions a few hundred yards away to the rear.

The new hill seemed nicer and more restful, with no snipers. We were at platoon strength and I was still the runner. My bunker overlooked the paddy fields beneath, guarding the track leading down to the platoon HQ and signals bunker. The platoon sergeant was a regular soldier as were most of the old hands. They had been in action in the Middle East prior to being drafted to the Arakan, and their experience was vital to us younger soldiers.

Since the new hill was further away from the Japanese, we had time to prepare our position. Around the hill lay the debris of war: empty ammunition boxes, steel helmets, cardboard, cases and old newspapers. Some of it was from the British retreat of a year ago, when an advance had failed and the monsoon had forced both sides into a stalemate in the flooded paddy fields. I decided to set up a dummy machine gun post using two wooden ammo boxes and some bushes with a dummy cardboard barrel thrusting out of them. Although a Heath Robinson contraption, it would appear effective to any advancing Japanese soldiers, or at least make them think twice, giving me a chance to get a shot in first. I completed it by creating a dummy head of white paper finished with one of the old steel helmets. At night we would cover up surrounding tracks with bushes in order to confuse any Japs or at least hold them up for a short time. The next day, the Company Commander, Major Shaw, inspected our position and praised our work.

Water was at a premium in our new position as there was no natural supply. One of the old hands soon showed us how to get some from the dry paddy. He dug a round hole three foot wide by two foot deep at the base of a hill. That afternoon the hole was empty, but by the next morning it was nearly full of very clear water, gallons of it. It had filtered through during the night. Some of the men had dug up turtles while extending and preparing old bunkers and one old hand dumped them in the water hole to keep it clear of insects. Basic but simple.

Many strange things happen during war. We were overlooking another foothill and we began to see cattle feeding on a nearby dried out paddy and surrounding weeds. Young village lads about ten or twelve years old were herding the cattle close by. While we were filling our water bottles they approached us, carrying bunches of bananas and *jaggery*, a form of toffee wrapped in palm leaves, and tried to sell us some. The bananas were wild ones with seeds in that could jar your teeth if you bit into them too hard. We admired the bravery of these young lads. This was the front line, with both sides ready to fire at any time, and all they could think of was selling their wares. They made several trips to our lines selling things. On one occasion they offered six-foot sheets of bamboo matting for sale. Some blokes bought them to sleep on during the two-hour rest periods in guard duty.

Our hill was alive with wildlife. There were all sorts of animals, including wild jungle fowl. One of these birds really scared me one night. It strutted through the dark leaves and rubbish up the hill towards my bunker and I thought it was a Jap creeping about. It was funny really, my eyes straining in the darkness to see who was there and my finger on the trigger, waiting to shoot, but I couldn't see anything. I just heard these footsteps turning round a couple of yards or so away and going back down the hill, crumpling the leaves as they went. It was the next day, when I saw the jungle fowl strutting up and down the hill in the same manner, that I realized what it was that had cost me a night's sleep.

Another night I heard a rustle of movement in bushes down in a hollow among trees. One of our chaps was sleeping in a bunker above the hollow. I reported it to the sergeant, suggesting I should throw a grenade in case it was the enemy. He agreed. Unfortunately, the grenade hit a tree and dropped on to the roof of the bunker where the chap was sleeping and then rolled off in front it, where it exploded with a loud bang. I'd started something. I heard our sergeant talking on the phone; he said the CO wanted to know why a grenade was thrown and had ordered us all to stand to and await an impending attack. Most of the men were awake by now. I moved around to alert them. Two men challenged me to halt and give the password. I gave it, and one of them said that I was lucky. His friend was going to shoot me, but had recognized me just in time. In a rush to obey the order I had not put my steel helmet and hadn't heard their first low-key challenge. The tommy gun that would have blasted me away was now pointing safely at the ground, and I returned to my position and stood to for an hour. The order then came to stand down as no attack had taken place. The next morning I got a load of stick from everybody. They had lost their sleep through me. I was still learning. Next time I would wait before wasting a grenade.

Later, I explored the hollow from where I had heard the noises that night. Some thought it had been a bear and they set a trap with bedding rope and bully beef. The bear found the tin and the men pulled on the rope attempting to spring the trap. Fortunately, the ropes broke and the bear escaped. It was a good job, really, as no one had given any thought to what they'd have done if they had caught it.

We moved on, advancing across the Arakan. I was ordered to

guide a party of men back from C Company to BHQ. The officer gave me the route I had to follow, but it seemed wrong to me. There was an easier, more direct route bypassing our old abandoned C Company position. In that climate, with heavy packs and full gear, the men would be very hot and tired if they had to cover that extra ground. But being a good soldier, I stuck to my orders in spite of the barracking I got from those in the party that knew the route. After a hot and sweaty journey through scrub and paddy fields we arrived and reported to the officer waiting for us. 'Good. I see you didn't come through the minefield then', he said. The old route had been booby-trapped and no one had told me!

Our next detail was to spend a few days guarding the guns that were blasting the Japanese positions on the Mayu Range. We moved behind Brigade HQ, a group of us settling into an area the size of a football field, with jungle-covered mountains towering in the background. On both our right and left flanks were walls of thick thorn bushes around fifteen feet high and to our front there was a road. Flanking the thorn hedge between Brigade HQ and us was a small jungle gully blocked with large lumps of rock at each end. We were here for a day or two's rest, with the somewhat easier task of guarding the guns from parties of Japs, as opposed to front line fighting.

We learnt that some seven thousand Japs had infiltrated the Arakan, threatening to push the 5th Indian Division back to the Bay of Bengal. This would have been another 'Dunkirk'. But we pitched our two-man tents in the open, as we felt we were far enough behind the front line that there was no need to dig trenches for what would be only a short stay. We wrote some letters and were able to scrounge extra food and beer and take things easy.

That evening we saw a lot of campfires up on the distant hillsides and a weaving line of flaming torches moving down towards us, but we didn't believe this was anything to worry about and went back to our tents to sleep. We slept fully clothed, with our packs for pillows and our rifles, ammunition pouches and other weapons at our sides, but we felt so safe that we took our boots off. The bright moonlight and the knowledge that guards were patrolling up and down our tent lines helped us to relax, and I slipped into a deep sleep. I was dreaming of the noises of war when I suddenly woke to find the crack/pop of Jap rifles, the crump of grenades and the light machine gun fire was for real. I quickly put my boots on, prepared my rifle, set my bayonet and got ready to stand to. There was no panic. We were now hardened soldiers and instances like this were a matter of routine. The sergeant major gave the sentry a right dressing down for not alerting the men earlier and ordered us into the nearby *chaung* gully near the thorn hedge. A couple of Bren guns were set up at each end, with an all-round defence by other weapons, to try to secure the area. We were each given four grenades and crammed into the gully, leaving our tents in the open ground. We were thankful for the thorn hedge as it appeared that most of the battle was taking place on the other side of it, at Brigade HQ. No one seemed to notice us, so we held our position.

Suddenly a soldier raced up from Brigade HQ shouting for the infantry; he was promptly arrested for leaving his post and put under escort within our gully, to be returned to his unit and charged. We waited for the Japanese to attack our position, but the fighting petered out and we stayed in the gully until daybreak.

The Japanese had retreated back up into the mountains. Later, artillery spotters located them and started blasting their positions on the mountain side, the 5.5-inch guns giving them a heavy barrage of 100lb shells, turning their green positions to a dirty brown in a matter of minutes, with clouds of dust and landslides, to deter them from attacking again. 'No rest for the wicked', one bloke said, as we set about packing up our tents and prepared to move to a more secure position. Unfortunately, the guns were only a few yards from our tents and fired a shell every half hour or so throughout the night. We couldn't sleep at first, but after a couple of days we got used to it and managed to sleep throughout the shelling.

My running duties continued. Once, when I was taking a message, I took a track at the base of the hill and noticed an area of disturbed soil on a bank between two lush green areas. I approached it walking casually, but as I got to the pock-marked bank, I sprinted through and kept running. A Jap machine gun fired at me just a second or so too late. This machine gun was fixed in position and sighted to that small area of disturbed soil, so was not able to follow me. I delivered my message to Major 'Bobby' Shaw further up the foothill and returned down the forward slope at speed to the safety of the *chaung* and the banana grove, then went back to BHQ for a meal and rest. I had to keep my wits about me all the time and made many more runs playing chicken with these particular Japs. They must have known I was there, but never got me.

The scrublands bordering the paddy fields were covered with waist-high weeds. The heavy dew would soak my trousers as I pushed my way through them. The sun beat down on my steel helmet and beads of sweat trickled down the sides of my face. My jungle-green shirt would be wringing wet. The Lee Enfield rifle slung over my shoulder seemed to weigh a lot more than its 10lb as I walked through towards the foothill where C Company had dug in. The Japs were on the opposite hill and snipers were scattered around the paddy fields. I felt very much alone and scared as I got nearer. I remember one occasion, whilst on my way to C Company, when suddenly everything went quiet. The birds stopped calling, the lizard with a call that sounded similar to a swear word was silent and all animals seemed to disappear. Then a screaming shell smashed into the paddy fields between the two hills, sending up a geyser of smoke and mud. As luck would have it, C Company's position included a *chaung* with four-foot high banks and wild bananas growing in water which led right up the hill to where they were. After the shell dropped I took off for this cover, and more shells crashed down around me. I leapt down the bank to find myself ankle-deep in water but safe, and headed towards our hill. Flying metal from the shells chopped through the banana leaves above my head, showering vegetation all around me.

I waited in the *chaung* until things had quietened down, then worked my way up through a gap I knew to the lower position where Colour Sergeant Jack Eves and the Company cooks were, at the base of the hill in a high-banked, tree-covered gully, just off the *chaung*. They were old hands from the Middle East battlefields. They suggested I waited for a while until the shelling stopped and they calmly played cards on a makeshift table and wooden boxes around the cookhouse area. We all sat there as pieces of metal ripped into the trunks of the trees and branches around us. I watched as a large piece of shrapnel flew towards me. It was like slow motion. It made a strange buzzing noise and embedded itself into a tree inches above my head. I couldn't have got out of its way. Later, as things calmed down, I raced up to Major Shaw's trench and finally delivered my message. After handing over a message my habit was to go the quickest way down a forward slope at a run, but sideways to keep my footing. I had done this for some days without trouble so off I went from C Company. Halfway down I heard a bang, and a bullet kicked up dust on the slope about a foot away from my feet. I stumbled with shock but kept going. The crack/pop of yet another Jap rifle followed me, but by then I had the protection of the *chaung*. Vowing to change my habits next time, I raced back to BHQ a lot faster than I had gone out. A day or so later, I was relieved from my running duties and sent back to C Company on the hill. It didn't last long. Two weeks later, the chap who took my place went missing. They decided to make me the runner again, and now it was my full-time job.

During the end of January and into February 1944, we moved on to a new foothill and watched an air-supported infantry attack aimed at clearing a main Japanese defensive foothill nicknamed the 'Tortoise' because of its shape. Many attempts had already been made to capture it from the Japs. In the past days barrages of 5.5-inch shells and 25-pounders had turned the foothill from green to a barren brown, and at times the entire area would disappear under clouds of dust.

Vengeance dive-bombers had been called in and a group of these flew up and over, appearing to have passed the foothill as they climbed high in the sky. They then circled and came screaming down straight at the foothill, releasing their bombs on the enemy positions. Once more, clouds of smoke and dust would hide the horror beneath. As the dust and smoke settled, a burst of fire would be heard as the Japs let us know they were still in business. Liberator heavy bombers were also used to break down the Japanese by relentlessly pounding them.

At BHQ, we were asked to watch out for the aircraft recognition panels of cloth that our attacking soldiers would put out when they had captured the Tortoise. This was to stop further air strikes on our newly held positions. About an hour later we saw small figures in the distance laying out the cloth, and a huge cheer went up.

Although the dive-bombers helped us, we also had a lot of air support from two Spitfires. We nicknamed them the Maungdaw Twins. These two fighters flew over our positions every day, supporting the ground troops. On one occasion we saw enemy planes fluttering down out of the sky like leaves. It was claimed that the Spitfires had shot down fourteen Japanese fighters in a spectacular dogfight. Earlier in the campaign I saw the same two Spitfires flash overhead, heading home full out, pursued seconds later by Jap fighters recognizable by the large red suns on their silver wings and fuselage. No one fired. They were all out of sight in seconds.

One day the Signals Officer, Captain Topham, called me and said that I was to take a message to C Company on a foothill very close to another in a distant paddy field. The two hills were almost identical. In order not to lose my way I decided not to use the cover of the trees, bush and weeds, so that I could keep a constant eye on my destination, even though I would have to go in a straight line towards the hill and risk landing in enemy hands. Off I went, straight across the dry paddy fields, hoping that no Jap snipers or patrols would spot me. I arrived safely at the base of the hill and stood and listened at the bottom of a small track leading up into the jungle scrub of the hillside. Then I heard people talking. Thinking it was C Company, I moved up the track. I bumped into four Indian soldiers in a weapon pit with a large radio set, all dressed in British jungle-green uniforms. Straight away I took them for some artillery operational unit of our Brigade and asked them in English if the Royal West Kents were on the hill anywhere. They looked very worried and didn't speak but just shook their heads and packed all their equipment away. I felt uneasy and decided not to hang around but retraced my steps back down the hill. I had just reached the foot of the hill when I met Captain Watts leading a group of C Company men in my direction. 'I see you have got to the hill before us, Private Street', he said, grinning at me along with all the others. This embarrassed me, so much so that I forgot to tell him about the group of Indians and their radio. Later, we heard that units of the Indian National Army or JIFFs (Japanese Indian Fighting Force) as they were known, were probably operating against us in this area, fighting with the Japs. Anyway, I passed the message over to Captain Watts and headed for BHQ, wondering whether I'd had another near miss and thinking myself lucky to be alive.

The battalion moved up to a forward position and awaited darkness. When it arrived the mist fell. We then advanced on to the paddy fields, passing Japanese positions on the jungle-covered foothills. During the first hour a lone sniper opened up with a light machine gun, probably hearing rather than seeing us. His tracer bullets floated high over the column and off harmlessly into nowhere. There was no panic. We just kept marching at the same pace, moving deeper into enemy territory and leaving the sniper behind, but marking his position for others to deal with later. We pushed on to our objective and at first light we dug in on the paddy fields near a village by the Naff River. Whilst there, Lieutenant Tom Hogg, a B Company officer, used gun cotton with short fuses to do a 'spot of fishing'. We needed to improve our supplies and that was the quickest method.

We infiltrated twelve miles behind the Japanese lines. Some of our own Indian troops were to take a village with us in support. The Indian troops attacked the village just before first light with artillery support and air strikes. We consolidated our position and waited for further orders. The battle was raging, with the crump of mortar bombs and grenades and the crack/pop of the Jap rifles all around. The heavy bursts of the replying Bren guns could be distinctly heard. We could see some of the *bashas* (huts) on fire, others smoking. Then the Signals Officer called me, pointed to the burning village and told me to find my Company position. I collected his written message and set off across the flat paddy fields towards the palms and other trees around the burning chaos in front of me. I hadn't much of a clue where to find them.

As I reached the village, things looked worse than I'd thought. I began meeting panic-stricken villagers, men, women and children, pale with fright, fleeing from the battle-torn area. I could hear grenades going off and mortar bombs exploding, together with machine gun and small-arms fire, but I couldn't find C Company and so headed for the road that led straight into the village centre. When

I got there I spotted some Indian soldiers running around among the burning huts. One dashed out of the smoke and on to the road. The wild-eyed Indian with his fixed bayonet glared at me, but I calmly asked him if he had seen the West Kents around. He looked at me as if I was mad, shook his head as if he didn't understand and dashed back into the smoke. I continued along and out the other side of the village, on to a built-up road passing through open paddy fields. There was a large iron bridge several hundred yards in front of me and I spotted distant movement on it. This was the bridge over the Naff River. I hesitated but decided to check it out, as I thought it might be C Company. If not, I would go back into the village. I slung my rifle and started for the bridge. The road was six feet higher than the paddy fields, and thick bush, rushes and weeds bordered it on each side. Now I could make out matchstick-sized figures in the distance and I realized that they had seen me and were taking up positions of defence. They were Japs, and I'd come too far and ended up behind enemy lines. I slowly turned and walked off in a normal fashion, eventually making it to a safe distance, out of range of the enemy guns.

I then approached the burning village for a second time. As I looked up I heard the roar of an aircraft and machine gun and cannon fire, and saw a Jap plane blasting the side out of one of our Spitfires. As the Jap peeled off, the Spitfire trailed black smoke and eventually crashed near another village on a distant paddy field. After further searching I eventually located my Company, well to the rear of the village, and delivered the message. The fighting continued, and the Japanese eventually retreated to the large iron bridge on to which I had nearly blundered.

Fire was a continuous hazard in the long, hot, dry periods in this area of the Arakan. Near our position there was a small river flowing through the paddy fields, surrounded by an area of bush and jungle-covered foothill positions. A fire started in the bush on one occasion, probably caused by mortar shelling. This drove a mixed bag of Indian, British and Japanese soldiers off their foothills. Our Company cooks had just prepared dinner as the flames started burning trees and bushes around their position. They were ordered to leave for the nearby river and shelter until the fire had passed, so they dropped the dixies or food containers with the dinner in them down into deep slit trenches to prevent them from being burnt. When they returned they served a late dinner, still hot, kept warm by the fire. During this mayhem we all started to cut fire-breaks in the area around, sometimes having to dash and take refuge in the river as sparks and embers settled on our packs. Luckily we were wearing steel helmets, but many were burnt and had to jump into the nearby water. The war stopped for a short while, as friend and foe fought nature rather than each other. Eventually, wind- and fire-breaks were completed and the fire burnt itself out, leaving charred foothills baring their black peaks and clouds of smoke all around. Our positions and those of the enemy were reoccupied, and the business of war resumed.

I returned to BHQ for more work and heard that the fire-ridden village had eventually been taken by our troops a day or two later. We heard that some more mail had arrived and I eagerly moved forward to collect my letters and a bundle of newspapers. In a quieter moment I started to read the newspapers in my trench, but it was early evening and the sergeant ordered us to stand to. He said, 'Another day tomorrow, Street, to read your papers. Get on with the job in hand.' I put the papers down and leant forward in a position of readiness, rifle and bayonet resting on the parapet of my trench. Another night without sleep was ahead, two hours on and two hours off guard throughout the hours of darkness, and for all the nights to come. I looked out on to the now darkening paddy fields with mixed feelings and a touch of homesickness.

As darkness fell the noise of frogs and insects took over. My eyes strained into the dark as I watched the track for signs of any danger. This was our way of life now and for many months to come. As dawn approached, part of the night-time sky lightened. This brought relief to men who were forcing themselves to stay awake after days of lack of sleep and nights of guard duty; we were now almost at breaking point with exhaustion. As the sun rose, a quiet order to stand to was given. Men still asleep were shaken awake to take up positions of defence all over the hill. But it was a quiet morning. We were on the offensive with fixed positions for a few days. We were more relaxed as we were now chasing the Japs, rather than they chasing us.

We moved to a jungle-covered foothill almost as high as a tower block, standing in the paddy fields like some castle which would be protected by its moat in the rainy season. It was covered in straw-coloured rice waiting to be harvested. This foothill was typical of the many stretching away into the distance to meet the Mayu range of mountains that seemed to reach up to the sky. After standing down, we checked weapons and performed other routine tasks. These were all the things that had been neglected when the enemy were chasing us. We had no time then.

Here at BHQ the Signals Platoon enjoyed a cowboy's breakfast of baked beans and tinned bacon, with hard biscuits and a cup of tea. As they ate breakfast some signallers were already working, contacting the rifle companies and radioing through the orders for the day. 'I say again, Able, Baker, Charlie, Dog. Come in please.' The noise continued to drone into the warm air as others rested, ate and dozed away when their meal was over. The work of the day went on and a call was heard for one chap or another to attend to some routine duties, but I continued to rest. This was short-lived, however, as I was called over by the Signals Officer to take a message to C Company. I moved down the track to the paddy fields and on into knee-high weeds, not relishing another day of wet feet and for perhaps an hour or two an unknown future. I ran quickly to some distant foothill where C Company was dug in, but again I was lucky and once again I survived unscathed, my message safely delivered.

The weather was extreme. An early morning mist and heavy dew would leave the area soaking wet. The high humidity would drench my clothes, and my feet would be wet through. Once the early morning mists lifted, the hot sun would soon dry us out. Then our uniforms became drenched with sweat. One night we had a real tropical storm. We runners were busy putting up rough shelters over our rest area, using branches or whatever was available. Suddenly John Harman, from D Company, appeared with a patrol. He suggested I used banana leaves to make the roof more watertight. We did, and it worked. Although none of us knew this at the time, John would go on to show extreme gallantry at Kohima, but was unfortunately killed. He was awarded the Victoria Cross posthumously.

Some time later, whilst delivering a message, I was following a small high-banked stream at the side of the paddy fields. I was taking my time, watching mudfish skip down the muddy banks of the streams and dodging eel holes full of water which moved up and down, showing that the eels were at home. (The locals would tie a maggot to a piece of string and leave it over one of these holes, waiting for the eel to take the bait. When the bait disappeared into the hole, the string was pulled out with the eel attached. It was like pulling a cork from a bottle. Later, when the war had ended, we tried this method. We gave those we caught to the young Burmese children watching us.) I entered a *chaung* leading to our foothill, through a gap in the high bank used by Company cooks to get water for the evening hot meals and tea. Soon I left the ankle-deep water, moved out into semi-dry cover in the weeds and scrub on the edge of sun-dried, unworked paddy fields and quickly crossed an open area on the way to BHQ. Near the edge of the paddy, I stopped near a *bund*, where I saw the figure of a soldier coming towards me. I hid behind the *bund*, readying my .303 rifle and focusing it on him. After a moment he came into full view, at which point his English-shaped steel helmet and his jungle-green uniform gave him away, and I recognized him. He was the A Company Runner.

We chatted for a few minutes and he suggested that we sit down and have a smoke instead of rushing back. It seemed a good idea. He placed his netted steel helmet between his feet and rested his Thompson machine gun between his legs, holding the pistol grip with one hand and lighting our cigarettes with the other. Everything was quiet and peaceful, the calls of doves, jungle birds and insects could be heard, as we relaxed with our smokes. I had done my job, delivered my message and was on my way back to BHQ for a welcome rest. Suddenly his gun went off, thankfully only a single shot instead of an automatic burst. He had inadvertently squeezed the trigger. It made a hell of a racket in the quiet jungle and the bullet tore into his helmet and rattled around until it came to a standstill. Neither of us was injured, and the bullet eventually ended up as a flattened lump of metal trapped in the helmet netting. We immediately took cover in the surrounding scrub and made our way back to BHQ.

Our regiment continued its push forward towards the Mayu range, an unforgiving place which was difficult to map properly. It was a maze of small peaks and thick jungle, with a network of dry *chaungs*. Off the road, most paths were game tracks made by wild animals. We could hear them at night.

The carnage of war was everywhere: dead bodies in differing stages of decomposition, some stripped to skeletons by the animals and insects of the jungle. Weapons and equipment lay strewn all over the place. Whilst moving down a *chaung* with a message I found a brand new Japanese helmet with cover and net. I looked at it for a few minutes trying to decide whether to keep it or not, but souvenirs of any weight or size were a burden, so I left it where it was.

The Japs had dug in well on the ridges above the Tunnels, but we infiltrated their positions one night, moving through the paddy fields. We walked in the darkness in single file, our mules loaded with supplies, ammunition and equipment. We marched all night past foothills and through dry paddies. It was now mid-March 1944. As dawn broke over the misty fields, one of the mules let out a loud braying noise and the others joined in. At the same time, someone saw a Jap dashing away into the bush and then into the jungle at the edge of the paddy we were crossing. We halted and had started to organize defensive positions when the first Jap 75mm shell screamed over our heads, landing on the BHQ area behind us. About thirty shells fell, mostly to our rear. We scraped out shallow trenches in the rock-hard ground of the open paddy field, sweating in the heat of the morning sun. There was a rumble of guns as our artillery spotter eventually pinpointed the Jap gun, and our own shells came over our heads with a loud, burning, whispering sound. The bangs of their explosions somewhere in the hills in front of us quietened the Japanese artillery and no more shells were fired at us. We had suffered losses, including John Topham's batman, and this upset Topham a great deal. The chap who had replaced me as C Company runner was also injured. The next day, B Company led the advance and asked for artillery support to soften up the enemy, but unfortunately our shells fell short. The guns fired at least two rounds before they were silenced and that was by word of mouth (the radio was damaged by the first salvo). There were seventeen killed and a further forty-one wounded.

C Company prepared to move further forward. I was now the Company Runner again, replacing the wounded chap. We moved to a ridge-like foothill with BHQ Company. Here there were several old Jap foxholes, all in a line, dug about two feet lower than the track. When we struggled in through their small oval entrances, built into the cliff-like sides of the ridge, we found each foxhole had been enlarged to take three men, able to lie side by side. The roof was very close to our heads. It was very claustrophobic, so I made sure that I would be the last man in and thus near the opening, when we used them to sleep in at night whilst on guard. The next day, we moved to another position and stayed there for a few days. I would take messages to and from the Company whilst they dug into their new positions. My run-routes went past the remains of the blown-up metal bridge that spanned the River Naff.

As a runner for C Company, attached to the Signals Platoon of HQ Company, to be shot at by snipers and experience near misses from shell fire out on open paddy fields was all part of the job. This was now my third stint as runner. The others had all been killed or wounded. One was found in a minefield next to the body of a dead Jap. Circling vultures drew the attention of the patrol looking for him. As time went by I got more used to being a runner and more relaxed, even taking the opportunity to pop in and look at a deserted Japanese roadside cookhouse, later to be occupied by BHQ, on the side of the road leading to the Tunnels. I wandered off the road into the cookhouse to look for anything that might be of value or interest, but I only found a pair of old wooden sandals that were of no real use, so I threw them away. When I turned round I was quite shocked to find I was looking into two foxholes on either side of the track that I had just come down. If they had been occupied I would have been shot in the back. I investigated the foxholes further and found that they led out to either side of the road and back into the cookhouse. If you chased an enemy through one he could double back behind you.

We moved towards thick jungle and a mountainous area near the Tunnels. I moved up with BHQ, taking up positions in the bamboo forest at the side of a *chaung*, digging in a few yards from a bend in the dry riverbed. To our left was the road leading to the Tunnels about two hundred yards away. These Tunnels beneath the crest of the Mayu range were built for a forgotten railway to transport workers to harvest and export rice from the fertile Mayu river valley. When the builders went bust an all-weather road was laid. It was the only one in the Arakan capable of being used during a monsoon. The enemy now occupied the Tunnels and it was our job to get them out.

Behind the road was jungle. Our rifle companies were digging in on ridges close to the Japanese positions. High above us were well-defended Japanese ridges overlooking the Tunnels. The road had a dried up *chaung* to the right hand side, with a bed of small rocks and gravel and a six foot high bank up to the road itself, with jungle-covered mountains beyond. To the other side of the *chaung* was a bank of large rocks, three or four feet high, forming pools that stank of the dead fish which had been trapped as the river had dried up. This bank continued into the bamboo jungle.

The Japs would have seen us if we had gone any further. They controlled that part of the *chaung* and covered it with machine guns from the ridges above the Tunnels. One of our leading patrols had already run into some machine gun fire. A dead British soldier lay in the *chaung* where he had fallen. A Jap machine gun covered his body, perhaps for days, waiting for some of his comrades to come and move him. We waited where we were on our side of the bend. There was no hurry to leave the dried-up river bed, and we were well hidden. I crossed the road and ran down with the messages as some men repaired field telephone lines hit by mortar or shell fire. It was essential that any damaged lines were repaired immediately to maintain our lines of communication, and we worked continuously to keep things operational.

As we dug our slit trenches, several shells whispered over our heads towards the Japanese lines. A signaller hidden somewhere in the clump of bamboos started to operate his radio set: 'Come in Able, Baker, Charlie, Dog.' I was listening to the signaller's voice drifting into the still air in the heat of the *chaung* when the crack/pop of a Jap sniper's rifle sent a bullet whining down the *chaung* and a Bren gun answered with a short burst of fire. The mountains echoed with the thunder of shells exploding on the Jap positions near us. The signaller from the bamboo clump tried again to contact our rifle companies and eventually got through. The distant crump of grenades and light automatic fire told me that things were hotting up. Then someone called for the C Company Runner. Now it was my turn to take a risk again in the rainforests. As I got up I heard the crack/pop of a Jap sniper's rifle from the mountainside.

The Intelligence Officer, Brian Dungay, had to show me how to get to the new C Company position, and we raced across the *chaung*, me struggling to keep up with him. We climbed up the bank and across the road and dashed into the jungle on to an old track or game trail, following some lines of communication. We began to move up the mountainside among the trees and bushes, some with thorns that tore at our uniforms as we climbed higher. In parts the ground was soft, with a mixture of rotten leaves and stinking mud. The stench was worsened by the sweltering heat and an atmosphere like a Turkish bath. We were both soaked to the skin with sweat as we climbed. After we had climbed for a hundred yards or so, the ground levelled out to a row of bushes overlooking the road. The officer said, 'Keep your head down here, we are in full view of the enemy. If you look through the hedge you can see the Tunnels with the Jap positions on top.' We moved quickly past this hedge, taking a quick look as we passed. I nicknamed it 'The Privet' and it served as a landmark for me on future runs. Then we came across an area of trampled down trees, with football-sized balls of elephant dung and watery holes in the mud where their feet had sunk in. I nicknamed this area the 'Assault Course' as we had to climb over many tree trunks, some quite large. We continued to climb higher and then, to my relief, we started to go downhill and found ourselves back in another part of the *chaung*, with C Company dug in on a ridge nearby. The Intelligence Officer decided to stay at the position, turned to me and said, 'Well, off you go now Street.' I took off straight away, as this was no place to hang about, and with a quick look at the Tunnels as I passed the Privet, I soon arrived back at BHQ.

I was later asked to conduct a small mixed party of men to C Company. Some would stay and three others (from HQ) were returning. I was to guide them out and get back as quickly as possible for more duties. For the next few days I would do that little trip daily, taking messages, guiding groups of men to and from my Company position and helping to repair any telephone wire damaged by shells.

However, the first trip didn't go to plan. Off we went, with all going well, until I made the mistake of telling them that they could see the Tunnels from the Privet. I was shocked because they all took much too long about it, acting like tourists on a visit to a historic place. I had to be firm and tell them that the Japs could see them and we should get on our way as quickly as possible. We came to a fork in the telephone wire and for one moment I couldn't remember which direction to follow. The men started to pressure me, so I chose the left hand fork. I then felt I had made a mistake, but I was too stubborn to admit it and hoped the wire would lead to a *chaung*. On we climbed, up the mountainside. We were all soaking wet with sweat. Some men were swearing and cussing because of the arduous route. We eventually came to a twelve foot high dry waterfall and I knew now that this was not the right trail – but I dared not tell them, not yet anyway. We climbed the waterfall and continued about fifty yards higher up towards a thicket of high thorn that blocked the track. The end of the telephone line lay nearby. It was a dummy line. My comrades all looked at me with shocked expressions on their faces. We could hear voices behind the thicket and they were not speaking English. Some of my men were Cockneys and they didn't suffer fools gladly, but they didn't dare raise their voices. We quietly retraced our steps back to the fork in the telephone wires, took the right track and then went on to C Company. I left them there and returned to BHQ. They didn't think much of me as a runner and guide.

As the days passed, more and more people used the track past the Privet and more people looked over to the Tunnels. The Japs shelled the area twice one day. I had to go out with the signallers to repair damaged telephone wire on the track, but from then on I kept well clear of the Privet. In fact, I didn't hang round anywhere because Jap patrols were moving around in the forests nearby. It was a very dangerous area.

A group of our chaps brought in a Japanese prisoner of war wounded in the leg. We gathered round to have a look at him. This was the first prisoner we had seen in the three months we had been in action. He was a small man with a funny beard that ran under his chin like a chinstrap, but with no moustache. He looked dirty and dusty as if he had been in action a long time, very different to the photos Japanese soldiers carried of themselves looking neat, tidy and clean shaven in their uniforms. The MO and orderlies had to clear us away and they offered the Jap a cup of tea while the MO checked his leg. He didn't trust anyone and refused the tea. The Intelligence Section Officer came to help the MO and decided to move the Jap to a quieter place as many of the soldiers showed how hostile they felt towards him. He was sent further back into our lines to be looked after and questioned. Under the Japanese Army's code he would have been considered dead for allowing himself to be captured.

Our advance through the Arakan had cost us a lot of men. It was decided that fresh troops would finish the job. We'd had a lot of bad luck and, with the taking of the Tunnels in sight, we were replaced. I wasn't sorry to leave those hit and miss journeys up and down that dodgy game trail and was glad to be going. On my last run, I didn't even bother to look over the bushes that gave such a unique view of the Jap-held Tunnels, but kept well out of sight. I climbed over a four foot high tree trunk, the elephant manure and the watery elephant footprints of the 'Assault Course', and over the slope, still following the telephone wire until I met that dummy wire that joined it. I didn't make the mistake of following the wrong trail this time. I stuck to the right hand trail that led me down to another part of the jungle river where my C Company were dug in on the mountainside. I delivered my message and went back fast because, as previously described, these Jap-infested rain forests were no place to stick around. When I returned, I did take a quick last look at the Tunnels through the Privet. It was a Russian roulette kind of life that I had survived so far, and to safely complete that last run came as some relief.

Fresh troops moved into our rifle company positions towards the end of March 1944, and those of our men left moved out. They now had old men's faces, strained and tired under their tans. These were men that had lived a lifetime in a day and seen friends blown apart by shells whilst attempting impossible jobs. Nevertheless, we had advanced across and captured most of the Arakan up to the Tunnels before we left.

We watched our wounded come down from the rainforests and ridges and saw friends that we knew lying on stretchers. These included 'Happy' Hamstead from Pershore. I knew him from training days in Worcester. 'All right, Happy,' I said, as he passed. He smiled weakly. He lay belly-down on his stretcher while the MO checked his wounds. Happy had his back riddled with bullets from an enemy machine gun. I thought he'd died. It was only over fifty years later that I found out he'd survived. We had been in action a little over three months.

We moved into a large deserted village called Kanyindan to regroup, together with mules and muleteers carrying supplies from Rear Admin. Some sections were down to four men. We took over the village huts (or *bashas* as we knew them). I remained with BHQ Signals platoon, as C Company Runner. A big mule with a large radio set was unloaded for BHQ, and company telephones and telephone wire was set up all over the village. Our radio operator could regularly be heard at work: 'I say again, Able, Baker, Charlie, Dog. Come in, Able, Baker, Charlie, Dog. Come in.' He rattled persistently into the radio set as he tried to contact his rifle company's headquarters. We were allotted our huts, and I shared mine with other signals runners and batmen. Each of us had a bed space to unroll our bedding, one blanket and a ground sheet, and we left our packs, ammunition pouches and water bottles on top to mark our spot. We then got on with the business of settling into the camp. The cooks served a dinner of dehydrated potatoes, tinned mutton, peas or beans and some kind of sweet, all washed down with a mug of tea, which we all gratefully took back to our *bashas*. A few new replacements had arrived, mostly Welsh. They all seemed to be called Williams, Morgan, Davies or Jones. We had beer that night to get to know them better, ending in a hearty singsong. We were a good mix of Brummies, Welsh, Cockneys and Kentish men, with the odd Irishman, Geordie and Black Country chap. There were also some Jewish lads with us. Except for the odd crack/pop of a Jap rifle or the loud bang of a shell burst now and then in the distance, it was hard to tell that this area of jungle scrub, foothills and paddy fields was only just behind the front line,. We were back for a rest and we took things easy. Some of us got letters and parcels. I received a parcel of cigarettes and chocolate, but as I opened it I found that the chocolate bar had melted into a mass of silver paper. I managed to eat a little and shared some, spitting out the silver paper as I ate. We were given some extra airmail letters and cards to write home. That was a rarity, as was the extra beer and food.

Entertainment was provided sometimes. The Pioneers would build a stage for concerts or shows. We saw George and Beryl Formby at Dimapur once. They persuaded Beryl to pose on the back of an elephant. She was scared but she did it. The elephant sat down and she slid off. Of course everyone erupted with laughter. She wasn't pleased at all. But we did appreciate these performers. They had some bottle to come out and entertain us. It wasn't that far behind the front line. George Formby brought seven banjos with him, each tuned to a particular song. He'd dropped one and it was damaged, but Ivan Daunt, one of the Pioneers, repaired and glued it for him. It played perfectly.

At a later time, a mobile film crew put up a screen on a dried paddy field for a film show. It seems strange now that on that moonlight night, just behind the front line, we sat and watched a film. We felt a little uneasy at first. The Japs had been known to shell these film shows as they lit up the area in the surrounding darkness. But we soon forgot about that and sat down and enjoyed the film, then went to bed for a good night's sleep. Bill Cordwell (we called him Ernie), a corporal from BHQ, saw some Japs in the bushes watching the film. They must have been a forward patrol who had stumbled upon us. They didn't hang around, and one of our patrols tracked them down and sorted them out.

The next morning, someone discovered a large lake a few hundred yards away. After breakfast a group of us decided to set off for a swim. We chatted about what a good time we would have cooling ourselves down in the oppressive heat. We stripped off and dashed towards the lake naked like a crowd of eager school kids. We waded into the water and kept wading and wading, only to find that it was only a foot deep. It didn't get any deeper. Despite our disappointment, we made the most of it, splashing and cooling off.

I had nearly forgotten that I was still C Company Runner. I had spent most of one day resting in the shade of our *basha* when the NCO called for me and explained that O (Operations) Group had asked all officers to report to BHQ. I got that sinking feeling of dread about the future as I moved around to alert the officers. After a few minutes it was our turn to hear the bad news. We were to go back into action in north-east India.

We wrote our last letters home, starting 'Dear Mom, If you don't hear from me in the next few weeks don't worry', together with a few silly excuses that fooled no one at home; but we felt it best to try to cloud the real issue and not to let them worry.

We cleaned and fused our extra grenades, loaded extra Bren gun magazines and bandoliers of bullets and rations of food and moved out in Company formation. We rode in trucks with some ex-grammar school chaps from I Section, well spoken and rather posh to our minds, but good lads all the same. We had a singsong on the way to the airstrip. Then we filed on to the waiting Curtiss Commando aircraft. For many this was their first time on a plane, and it wasn't a good advert for flying. It wasn't very comfortable, there weren't any seats and we had to sit on our packs. The crew were Americans. The navigator kept poking his head out and telling us that if we saw any Japs we should put the Bren guns out of the windows and shoot them. That didn't do much for our confidence, but I couldn't see anything except trees and hills, then more trees and hills. The crew had parachutes but we didn't. When we asked why not, they said it was their plane! When we asked what we'd do if we had to bale out, the pilot said, 'You'll have to bale out won't you!' That wasn't much comfort.

Elsewhere, Tom Hogg went with our mules in British Dakotas. As soon as the Dakota engines roared into action the mules urinated everywhere. In the heat the stench was awful. The aircrew went mad. The urine collected beneath the floor of the fuselage amongst the electrics. I don't know how they got rid of it. It must have stunk for ages.

Although we were battle-hardened, little could have prepared us for what we were now about to face.

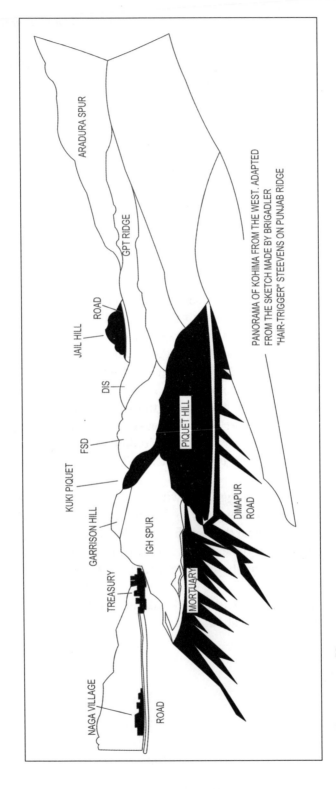

Panoramic View.

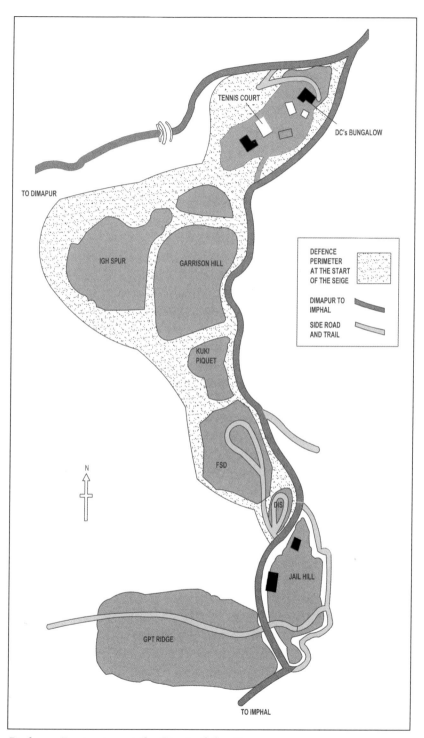

Defence Perimeter at the Start of the Siege.

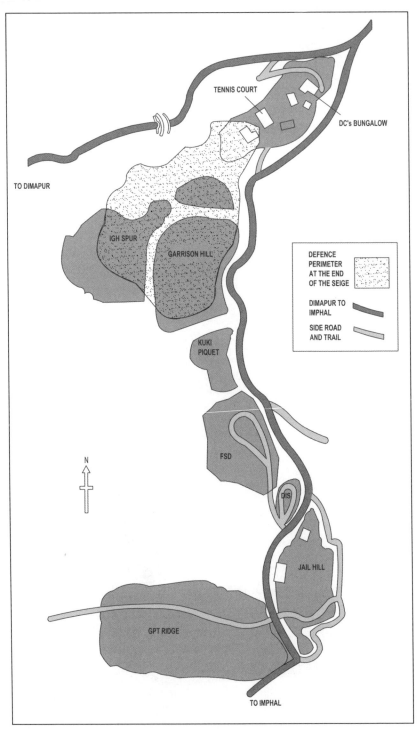

Defence Perimeter at the End of the Siege.

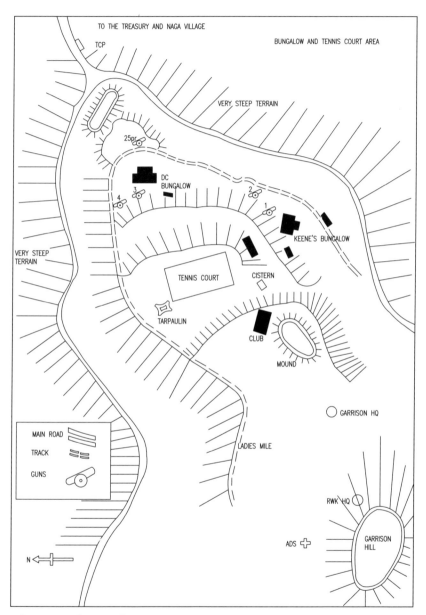

The Bungalow and Tennis Court Area.

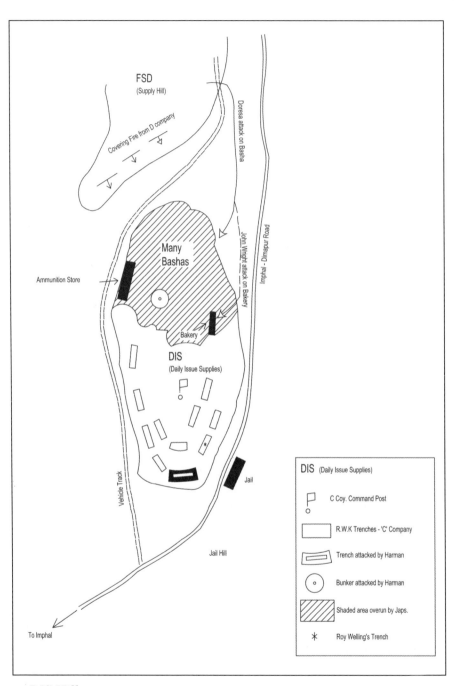

DIS Hill.

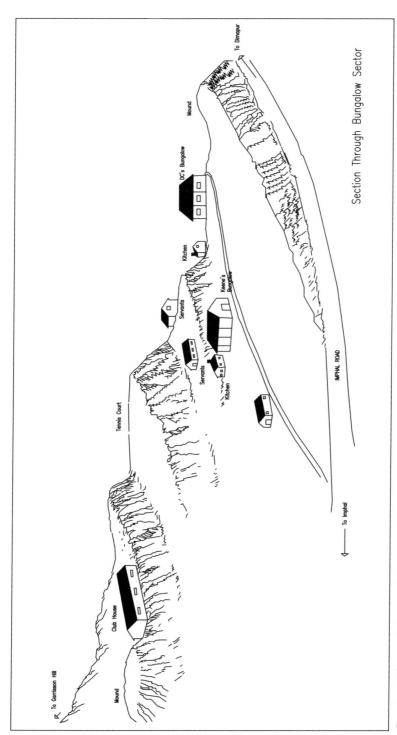

Section Through Bungalow Sector.

Chapter 4

The Siege of Kohima I
5–9 April 1944

We landed in India at the flooded airstrip of Dimapur and were piled into trucks that then headed up a winding hairpin road in the mountains towards Kohima, a small town in Nagaland, then a district of the north-east Indian state of Assam. We passed bewildered groups of Naga tribesmen, short sturdy hill people with a feather tied in their hair and a small pigtail near the nape of their necks. Many of them wore a red blanket on their shoulders and they appeared to us more like Red Indians than Asians. Some were carrying old shotguns and others had spears or bows, but all wore a Gurkha-style knife on their hip.

We reached Kohima and started to dig in. Then an order came saying that we weren't needed at Kohima, so after a few hours we headed back to Dimapur. It was only a small place then, but important because of its railhead for supplies to and from the rest of India. There we were put on standby and told to make the most of our short rest. We didn't get long and were soon back on the trucks going towards Kohima again. The air was cooler here. Perhaps we could dispense with our mosquito nets at long last. But that was to be the least of our problems, because as we got nearer to Kohima we could now see and hear shell bursts and mortar bombs and hear the crack/pop of Japanese rifles. We noticed some uniformed Indian deserters running back along the road shouting frantically, 'Jappi, Jappi'. They threw their weapons and bandoliers of bullets on to our trucks. We were angry when we saw them but we were told there was a roadblock further on and they would be stopped there and reorganized. We also passed trucks coming from Kohima, packed with men, some hanging on wherever they could. Others ran, trotted or walked. They all looked petrified. Most were non-combatants, such as storemen and clerks.

5 APRIL

The Japanese had launched an offensive from Burma. It was estimated that up to 100,000 men had crossed the Chindwin River to invade India. British military authorities had thought it was impossible for the enemy to bring any size of army through the dense, disease-ridden jungle and mountains, let alone such massive numbers. The defences around Imphal (the capital of the semi-independent princely state of Manipur, south of Assam, where British and Indian forces were gathering for a re-invasion of Burma), Dimapur and Kohima were apportioned accordingly. But the Japs had surrounded Imphal and sent their 31st Division north to capture Kohima and then Dimapur. Kohima was on the only direct road between Imphal and Dimapur. The town itself was 5,000 feet above sea level and set in a mountain range close to the Indo-Burmese border. The Japanese had to capture this town if they were to eventually take Dimapur and hope to successfully invade India.

Kohima was a forward supply depot and convalescent centre. At its central point was a road junction, from where roads and tracks led up to a garrison area, to the main town and to outlying villages such as Jessami. The men dug in around here, and the position stretched down a narrow spur of hills towards the south-east housing a convalescent hospital and some small metal-roofed wooden storage huts, workshops and so on. Further north among the trees was the Naga village. To the south lay the Deputy Commissioner's (DC's) bungalow, a small clubhouse and tennis court, with what before the battle were beautifully maintained gardens. Further south were Summerhouse Hill (also known as Garrison Hill) and the IGH (Indian General Hospital) Spur. Beyond this were a series of ridges and hills: Kuki Piquet, FSD ridge (where the Field Supply Depot was built) and DIS (Daily Issue Supplies) Spur which ran down towards the main road. Across the main road was Jail Hill and to the right was GPT (General Purposes Transport) Ridge. The whole area was covered with tall trees, but the vegetation was relatively sparse compared to the dense jungles and paddy fields of the Arakan.

The Deputy Commissioner's bungalow was situated on the lower slopes of Summerhouse Hill on a narrow strip of stepped terraces projecting to the north-east, enclosed by a hairpin bend of the Imphal–Dimapur Road. A track known as the 'Ladies Mile' ran parallel to the road, presumably used by colonial residents in more peaceful times to walk or ride and enjoy the picturesque views in the cooler mountain air. From the road a short macadam drive led to the bungalows of Deputy Commissioner Pawsey and Lieutenant Colonel Keene, the Commanding Officer of the Assam Rifles, who were based at Kohima; the kitchens and servants' quarters were on the terrace behind and above. Behind these and nearly forty feet higher was another terrace that housed an asphalt tennis court with a large tarpaulin water tank adjacent to one corner and a larger steel water tank near the other end, on a lower slope. To the west of the tennis court another terrace rose seven or eight feet, overlooking the court; but the north and south elevations fell steeply, forming the hairpin of the road below. Beyond this terrace was another, where a small clubhouse was built. Within the same terrace was a mound, thought to be man-made from works to the terraces and tennis court about seventy feet by twenty, a distinctive feature of great tactical importance as it looked over most of the eastern lower slopes. All the terraces were steep, and you couldn't see anything below unless you were near the edge; so when the Japs attacked (as described later) you could only see them when they came over the top.

Our lorries pulled up in a line, nose to tail, on the main Dimapur–Imphal Road just below IGH Spur and the men spilled out, leaving the main equipment on the trucks. The battle was already in full swing. Jap guns from the Naga village area were already causing problems. It was cloudy and misty when we got there so we reached our positions unhindered. But then the cloud and mist lifted. No sooner had the trucks stopped than the shelling started, reducing some of the lorries to blazing wrecks. The Indian drivers ran off back down the road where we had come from. The Garrison had one large gun, a 25-pounder, located by the Deputy Commissioner's bungalow. It tried to respond but only fired one or two rounds before the Japs took it out. A chap called Browning was manning it and he got hit in the head. (He survived the rest of the siege but was killed by a machine gun burst to the stomach right at the end, when we were being evacuated). Some men made daring and dangerous trips back to the lorries to get medical supplies and blankets which were in short supply from the start. Corporal Dennis Wykes (better known to his men as 'Bill') jumped off his lorry and dived straight into a drainage ditch. Bullets were flying everywhere and mortars falling all around. The mortars must have been close by, because you couldn't hear them coming. Men were hit as they got off the lorries, and the medics had to treat them in this shallow ditch with hardly any cover.

Almost 450 of us Royal West Kents came up to Kohima. Other troops of 161 Brigade to which we belonged were delayed, and by then the Japs had blocked the road, so they couldn't get in (although 161 Brigade eventually arrived at a village just north-west of Kohima called Jotsoma, where defences were erected and artillery support provided to Kohima). Not many of us were older than thirty-two, apart from some of the officers, and most of the latter were in their twenties. Some were younger than me, and I'd just turned twenty-four. We were split into six companies, A, B, C, D, HQ and BHQ, and detailed to particular hillside areas of the Garrison. A Company under Major Tom Kenyon and HQ Company set up on Summerhouse Hill (also known as Garrison Hill); B Company under Major John Winstanley on Kuki Piquet; C Company under Major Shaw on DIS Spur; and D Company under the young Captain Donald Easten on IGH Spur, to the west of Summerhouse Hill. As usual, I was the C Company runner attached to Battalion Headquarters (BHQ). The entire defended area was no more than 1,100 by 950 yards at its maximum. The Japs were already all around us.

The Pioneer platoon under Major Harry Smith, a former school teacher, were part of HQ Company and they set about constructing the Battalion Headquarters, organizing the cookhouse and the rest of the infrastructure that always appeared wherever we went. The platoon consisted of tradesmen: bricklayers, carpenters and a plumber. Les Crouch, Bob Clinch and Ivan 'Angus' Daunt were among them. Ivan and Bob joined up at the same time, together with Jack Eves, in July 1939 as militiamen. Ivan was granted a special wedding licence before they were shipped off to France. His son was three and a half years old before he saw him. Jack was a Colour Sergeant Major. He sorted out the cooks. He and Bob were good footballers and had represented the regiment, but their defensive capabilities would certainly be tested now. BHQ was set up between Summerhouse Hill and the Deputy Commissioner's bungalow in some old Garrison Headquarters Bunkers, a little above the Garrison Commander, Colonel Hugh Richards', Headquarters. Indian troops who were already defending Kohima before we arrived were pulling down *bashas* to give them a better line of fire.

It was early morning when Ron Clayton, D Company runner, and I started digging in behind a tree. When we had finished, Ron wasn't happy with it; he thought the tree didn't allow us a big enough field of fire and would give the Japs something to aim at, so we moved a little further up the hill and started digging again. I wasn't happy about this but went along with it despite the work we had already done. Afterwards we were worn out and lay in our trench to rest. Our redundant trench was in front of us now and beyond that a long curved trench, similar to those of the First World War. This housed the cookhouse, with its defences to the right. We runners were a few yards higher up, in three slit trenches. Behind us, in a big long bunker, was the Signals HQ under the command of the Signals Platoon Officer, Captain John Topham. Ernie Mason, B Company's radio operator, was in there busily testing his equipment to make contact with his company. A little further back and to our right, towards Summerhouse Hill, was the BHQ Command Post. In the pine trees alongside us an armoured car lay on its side, its weapon missing and its huge wheels motionless. Two chaps were detailed to smash it up later and push it into the adjacent *nullah* (ravine) so it was out of the way. The whole area had become cratered with small shell holes, and the litter and rancid smell of past warfare filled the air.

Our Commanding Officer was Lieutenant Colonel John Laverty. The men called him 'Texas Dan' because of his lean build and his hat. He always carried a six-foot bamboo staff to negotiate steep and rocky ground. His batman was Private Heffernan. They were both Irish, good friends and a right pair of characters. Heffernan always greeted everybody with 'Top o' the morning to you'. His experience of working in posh hotels before the war helped him in his role, but the CO had to pull rank on many occasions to shut him up. On arrival, lines of communication were set up to all the Companies, and Major Yeo of 24th Indian Mountain Battery could now direct his artillery with our 161 Brigade (located at nearby Jotsoma) from his position within the Garrison.

The enemy sent over barrages of shells that continued into the night and the next day. Joe Walsh, a young Irishman, was one of the first to be killed. One shell landed in our former trench behind the tree. This was too close for comfort, so we decided to dig deeper and widen the bottom of the trench so that we could both lie flat side by side. As I looked out of my trench, a chap standing in the doorway of a hut near a water tank suddenly disappeared as a shell exploded in front of him. The Jap guns must have been very near because you couldn't hear the shells coming. We called them 'whizz-bangs' because that's how they sounded. We only just had time to throw ourselves to the ground as the shells screamed down on us. The tree bursts were worst; the shrapnel would ricochet amongst the branches and rain down into the trenches below. Some of the troops used timber and the corrugated metal sheet off the *bashas* topped with soil to give head cover, but they couldn't do that in the forward trenches because they had to be ready for Jap infantry attacks. Some Indian troops located near us left their trenches and made an open fire, but the smoke drew more shellfire and scattered them quickly back into cover. They didn't do that again. One chap who was a bike rider kept his motorbike in the long curved trench by BHQ. It was virtually brand new, and I suppose he didn't want it damaged by shellfire. However, someone fell over it then chucked it out of the trench, and it was damaged in the next barrage. The rider was furious and laid into the chap who'd thrown it out. They were having a right set-to when an NCO broke them up, saying that we had enough problems sorting out the Japs, let alone fighting amongst ourselves. He could have put them on a charge but there was no point in that.

C Company was on DIS Spur that night and under mortar fire from the Japs. Five of the bombs landed near the platoon HQ. A corporal called Webber was told to get into his weapon pit and take cover. Just as he did so a mortar landed where he had been standing. He was lucky to get away with it.

6 APRIL

The morning of 6 April was sunny after a misty start. The mist had been thick and damp, and you could only see for about thirty yards. As the temperature rose the mist condensed and fell like rain from the surrounding trees, soaking everyone. In the early morning the Japs had taken Jail Hill and GPT Ridge. D Company tried to retake them but the enemy were too numerous, so they consolidated and dug in at FSD hill. This was a blow, because now the Japs were above us and could see C Company's positions on DIS Spur, although the tree cover helped at first. The trees were beautiful pines, lantanas, oaks and alders, but it wasn't long before all their foliage was blasted away and their trunks and branches split and splintered beyond recognition. I had to run messages through them exposed to enemy fire. There was very little cover. The Japs made the most of their position and fully established themselves on Jail Hill with extensive tunnels, some of which were extended with underground galleries, safe from the heaviest artillery and aircraft fire.

Most of my day was spent organizing and collecting mortar bombs and other ammunition that had been stacked near the roadside by the trucks. It was a hell of a job as Jap snipers were firing at us. Some Rajputs arrived, sent by 161 Brigade HQ now based in nearby Jotsoma. They were sent immediately to DIS Spur and dug in with the rest. These were the last troops to get through along the Imphal Road from the Dimapur direction. The Japs now closed the road and we were under full siege. The telephone cable lasted a further six hours before the Japs cut it. A detachment of 75th Indian Field Ambulance had also got through, commanded by Lieutenant Colonel John Young, a fair, slight, wiry man, who immediately took control of the disjointed medical facilities. He organized the construction of an Advanced Dressing Station (ADS) near BHQ, to replace five scattered Dressing Stations. There were lots of casualties before we got there, and the Dressing Stations were already overflowing. Something had to be done. Lieutenant Colonel Young could speak fluent Urdu and that was important in the ADS. With a chap called Barrett of the 1/17 Dogras (123 Brigade, 5th Indian Division), they organized some of the Indians and non-combatants to construct the ADS and do other jobs such as digging trenches to house the

wounded and burying the dead. This allowed some of the fighting
men to remain in their positions.

The Japs soon realized that we were not going to move. From then
on their attacks became more intense. The 4th Royal West Kent
Regiment held the main perimeter areas. Other troops helped defend
the Garrison: the Assam Regiment; the Assam Rifles; a company of
4/7th Rajputs; the 20th Indian Mountain Battery; a platoon of 2nd Field
Company, King George V Sappers and Miners; 75th Indian Field
Ambulance; plus other 'odds and sods'. These odds and sods, as they
were called, included soldiers from mixed units, some from the
convalescent or rest camps in Kohima, now trapped here with us.
Also trapped were many non-combatants. These were clerks,
storemen and other administrative staff. They weren't trained for
action and were an unfortunate burden. Some of them were very
scared. They had good reason to be. We all were. We were later told
that there were nearly 15,000 Japs out there, and we numbered a little
over 1,500 fighting men. 'Invicta' was the RWK regimental motto.
It meant 'Unconquered.' But things didn't look good. The
Unconquered, and the rest of the Garrison, were about to experience
their sternest test ever.

That night, the Japs directed a full-scale attack at C Company on
DIS Spur, commencing with a barrage from behind some buildings
on Jail Hill. George Martin was killed when a mortar landed on his
position. DIS Spur was a supply point, a small oval feature extending
to about 160 yards in length and about 30 to 40 yards wide in the
middle. The *bashas* still housed plentiful stocks of food and
provisions, together with ammunition. To the east side was a very
steep drop that bordered the main Imphal Road; to the south and west
were steep slopes from which the Japs would attack. C Company
occupied trenches, their position being some 20 yards wide at the
southern edge overlooking Jail Hill, from which they were separated
by the macadam Imphal Road. Major Shaw made us remove the
overhead cover to the trenches to improve our field of fire.

After the barrage stopped, the Jap infantry attacked. They didn't
make a secret of it. The moon was out and we could clearly see them
forming up on Jail Hill. They made a hell of a racket, blowing bugles,
screaming and shouting, psyching themselves up for the charge.

There was no doubt about it, we were scared. Then the training kicked in. We saw them come down Jail Hill and start to cross the road, approaching the steep climb to our positions. We held our fire till then. They were about 30 yards away when we let them have it. Artillery back-up from Major Yeo's 24th Mountain Battery guns based with 161 Brigade at Jotsoma was directed at the oncoming Japs, together with Sergeant King's (of the RWK) mortars. Roy Wellings, a corporal in 13 Platoon of 'C' Company, was in one of the forward trenches and King dropped in to get the 'lay of the land.' Wellings crept forward five yards, in the darkness, to the edge of the slope to spot the fall of King's ranging shots. King then phoned through to give the mortars their bearings. They were very accurate and had a devastating affect, killing and maiming many of the enemy as they charged. But they kept coming, wave after wave of them, rushing towards our trenches. We used rifles and grenades plus the Bren guns. We cut them to ribbons but they still got through, there were that many of them. Roy Wellings couldn't fire quickly enough. Despite hitting as many as he could, he was overrun. They ran past him towards the trenches beyond. He thought they might shoot him in the back but he couldn't look round. He didn't have time. He just continued firing and hoped those behind would deal with the others. They did, and the position was held.

The Japs then withdrew to regroup. Despite their losses they attacked again and again. At one stage Roy fell backwards and was bayoneting vertically as the Japs ran over his position. It was all he could do. Bobby Shaw, our Company commander, was hit in the leg after a tree burst by HQ. Privates Young and Sharpe were also hit; Shaw's leg was broken in several places. Corporal Day, one of the stretcher-bearers, took him to a *basha* and Captain 'Dodo' Watts took over. During the night, some Japs were heard digging in near to 13 Platoon. There were about 100 of them and they were only yards away. Led by Sergeant Tacon, with covering fire from Corporal Norman and Privates Dick Johnson and Ernie Thrussel, a group with small arms and grenades attacked and wiped them out. Corporal Webber was with them. His section killed loads. There was a lot of action around Company HQ; Captain Watts was hit twice in the arm and taken to the ADS. Liddell and Woodward were wounded, but Alf

'Ginger' Judges, one of the cooks, wasn't so lucky. He was killed. Sergeant Frank Bennett and Private Albert Paris were also killed that day. Throughout the action, Sergeant Stammers constantly visited his section posts, topping up their ammunition and giving words of encouragement to the men.

Acting Sergeant Pearman was in a trench with three others, so close to the Japs he could hear them talking and they could hear him. During the night a grenade rolled into the trench. The three other chaps got out straight away, with Pearman following behind. He threw himself out and down as the grenade went off, rolling out of the way while he saw flashes from a Jap's gun trying to shoot him. The others couldn't believe he'd got away with it.

Some Japs got into *bashas* housing ammunition stores in the middle of our position further up towards the top of DIS Spur. They must have sneaked round the west flank. We couldn't direct the artillery on to them in case it hit our blokes, so it was decided to wait until the next day to sort them out. When the rest of the Japs finally withdrew the hillside was littered with hundreds of enemy corpses, too many to count. Our losses weren't light. Jimmy Beames was in Roy Wellings' 13 Platoon. He caught a bullet in the shoulder but stayed at his post instead of going to the ADS. We couldn't afford to keep winning like this. We didn't have the men. It was hard to bury the dead. The Japs sniped at us and the ground was so hard to dig that you couldn't get very deep. Rigor mortis set in, and parts of arms and legs would poke out of the shallow graves. We buried men at night. The Japs left their dead until they captured the position and then burnt them. The smell of dead and burning flesh was terrible as it drifted across our lines. During the night they tried 'jitter tactics' to try and identify where we were. They would shout in English, 'Let me through. The Japs are after me.' No one replied. They even got snipers to fire single shots here and there, then awaited any response to try to assess the strength and position of our guns. We didn't take the bait.

There was a water tank close to my trench, a little way down the hill towards the tennis court. At least we would be all right for water, and that was a relief when I remembered what it was like at times in the Arakan. We had water for two days before the Japs shelled it. It was only then that someone decided to cover it with some camouflage netting. The water was still flowing through the pipe, but that only lasted a few more days before the Japs captured the reservoir nearby and turned the supply off completely. From then on water was rationed and thirst became a problem.

The shelling became more regular; the Japs let us have a barrage at first light and then at dusk, always followed by frenzied infantry attacks on the forward positions. We were lucky where we were, but the troops in the front line were involved in hand-to-hand combat each time they were attacked. It was calmer during the day, but we still had to be on the lookout for snipers and isolated machine gun and mortar fire. We had to be careful all the time. On one occasion we were sent scattering to the bottom of our trenches as a Jap machine gunner swept our area with indirect fire. It didn't last long. I don't think he had any particular target in mind, but was firing indiscriminately, hoping to catch us off guard. He nearly did. In a quieter moment, I looked around and saw some poor tethered mules, eating hay or straw, with large open wounds in their flanks. They didn't seem to be distressed and munched steadily at their hay, but later that day they had gone. I hoped that someone had cut them free.

The runs I had to make were different now. For a start they were shorter, and would become shorter each day as the Japs pushed us back. I had to take messages in the dark; it was too dangerous in daylight. Whilst taking one message at night, I followed a track over the back of our hill through Kuki Piquet down FSD Ridge to DIS Spur. The sound of someone digging close by alerted me so I slowed down, but it was too late. I was suddenly challenged by a voice: 'Halt.'

'Friend', I quickly replied.

The voice in the shadows growled, 'Password.'

My mind went blank. The password was 'Chowringee'. It suddenly came back to me and I said it quietly but eagerly, as to hesitate over a password could mean death. I reminded the men that I would be coming back that way, but their faces said it all: make sure we hear you and you know the password, or else you're dead. As it happened, these soldiers had just had a hard time, so I couldn't blame them. They were digging a grave for a dead friend and were on edge. It was as well I answered quickly, for they were in no mood for anyone like me playing silly beggars. The passwords used at Kohima often used the letter 'L', such as 'Lollipop' or 'Lilliput', as it was thought the Japs would have problems with their pronunciation. This would help the guards, especially in the dark. Also, some of the radio operators would talk in Welsh in case the Japs were listening. They were sure they wouldn't understand that. On one of the following runs, I noticed a case of whisky fastened by a padlock lying on the ground. I passed by and didn't touch it. Someone else did, though. When I went by the next day the case had been broken open and the lot had gone.

As the enemy tightened their grip, we were pinned down. We hadn't had haircuts for ages and because of the water shortage we were unable to wash or shave. We were always thirsty. We used an old fruit tin to urinate in and threw the contents over the parapet, and our redundant shell-holed trench for a toilet whenever we could. The whole area began to stink. During the night we got a shower of rain and caught about a pint of water in an old gas cape. We managed to get it into a container, but it was so bitter and the taste of rubber made it so sickly that we couldn't drink it for fear we would make ourselves ill. Disappointed, we returned to our trench. Luckily we were sitting down when some Japanese machine gun fire swept our position again. As the bullets zipped above us and into our parapet, I felt that our trench was taking the brunt of it. This went on for a several minutes, but we kept our heads low for the next hour or two just in case. For three nights running, a Japanese mobile gun had been sending shells on to our position. We would hear the gun approach, stop, fire its shells, then start up again and move to another position to fire at us again. It was on a road somewhere nearby and would keep moving so that our artillery couldn't get a bearing. This became nerve-racking as the engine turned over and then suddenly stopped. We knew that we'd soon hear the screaming sound of the shells. We immediately hit the bottom of the trench for cover. Each attack lasted for about half an hour.

7 APRIL

This was Good Friday. At home we used to have hot-cross buns, but here it was bully beef and biscuits. During the morning, D Company, aided by a platoon of sappers, were sent to assist with the removal of the Japs from the *bashas*, one of which was a bakery, around C Company. If they couldn't get them out, C Company would be cut off, overrun and killed, and DIS would be taken. It was that serious. Tree cover made observation difficult and the Japs had positioned some 75mm guns on the recently-occupied GPT Ridge. Lieutenant Peter Doresa was in charge of a platoon sent to the north-east of DIS to help clear the Japs from the occupied *bashas*. Captain Donald Easten set up a covering crossfire from some Bren guns, and with Doresa, Sergeant Major Haines led the platoon plus some Gurkhas, on a 40-yard dash uphill to the Japanese-occupied *bashas*. With bayonets fixed and throwing grenades they went, they ran straight into the enemy positions. Some *bashas* caught fire as the ammunition and explosives inside went off. Some Japs stayed inside fighting until they burned to death. Others ran out, some with their clothes on fire, and were cut down by Bren and rifle fire or by bayonets during the hand-to-hand combat that ensued. Sergeant Tacon manned a Bren further down the slope. As the fleeing Japs reached the edge of a terrace they slowed down and hesitated before jumping. He mowed them down there, and heaps of their dead littered the area. Tacon shot and killed fifteen the first night and twenty the next, with the corporal in the weapon pit above 'helping some more down the hill'. CSM Bert Harwood came over later to see Tacon and was amazed to find that he had a little white dog with him in his trench. He didn't know where he'd got it. He didn't care. He had enough to worry about, and left him to it.

 Ivan Daunt, one of the Pioneers, and others from HQ Company with some of the 'odds and sods' were deployed to assist C Company in positions overlooking the main road. The Japs sent some shells over and yellow smoke started to work its way up the hill. Some of the 'odds and sods' thought it was mustard gas and ran off. It wasn't. Later, there was a loud rumble and a number of horses and mules galloped past, immediately followed by screaming and shouting Japs. If the galloping animals were supposed to divert our attention, the noise the Japs made didn't conceal anything. In any event, the liberal use of grenades and small-arms fire stopped their progress.

The *bashas* were mostly of bamboo construction with thatched or corrugated metal roofs, but the bakery was built of brick around its ovens. The Japs used boxes and crates to construct defences and were well established in there. They were also among the trees, shrubbery and other huts and proved difficult to dislodge. They fired from between the crates and boxes and positioned a machine gun in the bakery doorway overlooking C Company positions. They had also captured some Indian troops and forced them to fire on us. Their weakest point was the eastern face, but this was where the brick ovens were. So Lieutenant John Wright in charge of the Sappers, and Donald Easten in charge of D Company, fixed bales of gun cotton to an old door taken from the Hospital, fused and charged it and ran it up the hill to the bakery. They wedged the door against the brick ovens, ignited the fuse and ran back to their position. A terrific explosion then took place, with bricks, timber, metal and provisions flying everywhere. The Japs ran out through the dust and smoke and were immediately cut down by C Company Brens and rifles. There was some close-quarter fighting as they desperately tried to flee; Easten just managed to shoot one Jap with his revolver as he got within a couple of yards of him. Nearly fifty Japs were killed. Not many escaped, and if they did they were certainly all wounded. Some of our chaps saw a wounded Jap fall as he was running off and went to take him in. As they approached he pulled the pin from a grenade and blew himself to pieces, wounding and killing some of his would-be captors. We had further losses, with Privates John Coleman and Joe Hesketh killed. They were both young kids, Hesketh being one of the youngest amongst us at just nineteen. After some close-quarter resistance two Jap prisoners were taken, the first ones to be captured here. They were both badly wounded: an officer who also had a broken leg died shortly after, a corporal lived a little over a week. Because of the disgrace he had already suffered in being captured he willingly submitted information. Although there was no interpreter, the Intelligence Officer somehow got details of the Jap positions and strength of numbers.

John Harman (some of us called him Jack) was D Company sniper and a pretty damn good one too. As a soldier he was first rate, very brave. It was he who carried 'Happy' Hamstead to safety when he was shot by a Jap machine gun. 'Happy' was one of the few who got close to him. He'd told 'Happy' that he had maps of sunken Spanish galleons in the Bristol Channel and suggested they hunt for treasure when the war was over. It was rumoured that he had been offered a commission but preferred to be one of the lads. That was strange really, because he was a natural leader, if a bit of a loner. Although everyone got on with him, he was too posh for most. Don't get me wrong, he wasn't a snob, but he was different to us. His father was a multimillionaire who owned Lundy Island. They even had their own coins and stamps.

John was older than most of us, nearly thirty, well travelled and well read. We'd be lucky to go to Rhyl for a day out, but he'd travelled the world. He had worked as a lumberjack in New Zealand and had done sheep farming in Australia. There wasn't much he didn't know about. I first met him at Market Rasen, at the training camp and he was with us at Allahabad when we came to India. I remember that when we were travelling on the train across India the rest of us would guess where we were. He knew. He had his own maps and a compass and had already worked out where we were and where we were going. He didn't make a fuss about it – it was just matter-of-fact to him. He was the only bloke I knew who had a bank account in India. His father set it up for him so he wouldn't go short. He even had his boots specially made. Some people said he had odd-sized feet and he had made up a pair to fit from two Japs he'd killed. I don't know about that, but 'Happy' gratefully accepted a pair after John had decided he needed a change, and he said they were all right. But John was superstitious. Apparently, he'd had his fortune read in Spain before the war and been told that he would live until he was seventy. 'Happy' was with him in Durban on the voyage out when John visited a Portuguese woman for a reading and was told once more that he would live a long life. One of our NCOs called Edmonds was with him at the hill station at Raniket when Harman asked an Indian fortune-teller to read his hand. But when the Indian looked at it he was visibly shaken and immediately got up and walked off, refusing to read any more.

Ivan Daunt knew him well and had some right banter with him. One time on the Arakan, Harman dropped in for a chat. He shouldn't have been there as it was nowhere near his company position. He was always where he shouldn't have been. Ivan teased him about his father owing Lundy, as Ivan's family lived in Starkey Castle in Kent. They didn't own it, they rented it, but Harman didn't know that. They talked about food or rather the lack of it. Harman asked if Daunt fancied some rice. He said yes, and Harman disappeared for a short time then returned with two sacks. He'd found them in a redundant Jap foxhole on one of his walkabouts.

Jack Faulkner, a lieutenant in A Company, couldn't work Harman out. The pair had to get past some snipers holed up on GPT Ridge. Faulkner ran out and heard the thud of a sniper's bullet behind him as he made for cover. When he looked around, he couldn't believe it: there was Harman casually walking with his hand in his pocket as if it was a Sunday stroll. He never got hit. The sniper never fired at him.

Despite his straightforward approach, there was a bit of the rogue in him. It was on the previously mentioned trip to the hill station at Raniket that he looked over the sheer drop at the edge of the road and spotted the tail of a snake. Without hesitation he immediately grabbed the reptile's tail, pulled it out of a crevice and shook it to death. He then paid a local Indian to make him a belt from the skin. On another occasion at Allahabad he caught a rock python, brought it in the barracks and let it wrap itself around some chap's bedpost. Then he woke him up. Well, as you can imagine, the chap went to pieces with panic. Harman simply grabbed the snake's tail and with a whip-like action rendered it lifeless. Another belt was made from the proceeds. He certainly had no fear of these creatures or indeed of any other animal. In fact, he was quite at home with them. On Lundy he kept hives of bees and was always out and about, happiest amongst the natural surroundings of the island. In India it was much the same. He'd often disappear on his own and go for a walk, even in the terrific heat of the midday sun. In the Arakan he would go out and return with *chapattis* or some other local produce that he had bartered for with the locals. On one occasion he returned with a young water buffalo because he thought a bit of steak would make a nice change for the lads. It did.

There was some talk of trying to get a patrol through to us from our own 161 Brigade in Jotsoma just outside Kohima, but the Jap roadblocks held everyone up. During the night, despite the shortage of fighting men, the Rajputs were withdrawn to Jotsoma via jungle tracks bypassing the road blocks. They took over ninety of the walking wounded out with them, together with about a hundred of the non-combatants, who had been just wandering about, often in the way and bad for morale. Major Peter Franklin and Lieutenant Colonel John Young, the MO, led them out. Ivan Daunt and some others went with them to help, but they all came back afterwards. We hoped they'd explain to 161 Brigade the alternative jungle route so we could get more reinforcements, but it didn't happen.

Straight after this we were finally cut off totally and surrounded. There was now no way in or out for our troops. The remaining wounded lay in long crawl trenches as the sick bay overflowed. They were in an awful state. Barrett and his Indians and other non-combatants dug more trenches for the injured, but they couldn't go very deep. It was difficult after about two feet because they hit rock, and that wasn't deep enough to protect them during the shelling. Many of the wounded got hit again or killed because of the lack of head cover. They had a bit more luck with the operating theatres. They constructed two and managed to get down six feet in one place. One had a timber roof, the other was just covered by a tarpaulin. Both were lit by hurricane lamps. It wasn't good enough but it was all they had. As soon as they were finished the doctors started to operate, with trestles and stretchers serving as operating tables.

When Barrett's men had finished digging the trenches, they helped nurse the sick and wounded, removing the dead from amongst them and then taking up the stretchers to bring new cases in. They were great. When rations were scarce, they gave up theirs for the wounded. When water was short, the wounded were given fruit or tomato juice from the Kohima Military Stores just to get fluid into them. They couldn't do without that. Barrett's men were very brave. They had to go all the way to DIS Spur to get the stored supplies, constantly under threat of enemy fire. Later, usually at night, they would help bury the dead. This had to be done quickly due to the accelerated decomposition as a result of the heat. The Japs' and our blokes' bodies were buried together, as there wasn't time to sort them out. Details of our dead were taken, hopefully to assist in recording things after the battle. They also had a hell of a time burying dead mules. The ground was so hard, but it had to be done. They couldn't be left to rot. Flies were everywhere.

With Captain Watts injured, Captain Tom Coath assumed command of C Company. We all liked him. Despite being an officer he seemed one of the lads. Ivan Daunt knew him before the war. He had been a salesman, and was a good rugby player too. On the boat out to the Middle East there was a rumour that Tom couldn't afford his mess fees. It was said that he was so well respected the men had a whip round to help him out.

Acting Sergeant Pearman was told to move to the flank of C Company on DIS Spur as it began to get dark. He had eight men in two groups of four. He went into a trench just off the track, with the others filing out to the trenches on the right. There was an explosion and suddenly Japs were all around them. Luckily, the Japs didn't see Pearman's men in the dark so they kept quiet. Pearman was well armed with a rifle and 150 rounds, a tommy gun with half a dozen magazines, six grenades and a Gurkha knife. Some Japs spotted the men at first light, but just stood there staring. Pearman shot them with the Thompson. One slid into the trench and Pearman shot him as well. There were still other Japs nearby; Pearman's men could hear them, so everyone kept quiet. They decided to make a run for it before the Japs found them, jumped out the trench and ran up the hill as quickly as they could. One chap got hit, but they all got back. The chasing Japs charged after them, but the Brens sent them scurrying back downhill. Now Pearman was in a trench with three young lads. He put one on guard so he and the others could rest. Within a few minutes the lad had slid to the bottom of the trench fast asleep. The same thing then happened with his replacement, so Pearman felt it safer to stand guard himself. He couldn't see anything in the dark so every half hour or so he threw a grenade to keep the enemy at bay. He slept as best he could during the day and resumed guard at night in the same manner. This carried on for several days until the position was relieved.

That night, the Japs attacked DIS Spur, mainly with 'jitter' and probing tactics to assess the strength of our positions. The attacks were hourly so no one got any sleep. They knew what they were doing. Yeo organized the artillery based outside Jotsoma to fire on to the Japs as they formed up to attack. That helped. Roy Wellings was in a trench near the edge of the road, and the chap beside him was already dead. He heard a noise but couldn't see anything in the darkness. There was a drop to the road below, so he half pitched and half rolled a grenade down the slope. As it exploded on the road below he saw the faces of the Japs who had been creeping up on him. The grenade put paid to their attack.

8 APRIL

On the morning of 8 April we awoke to be greeted by a machine gun that the Japs had managed to get on to DIS Spur during the night. This was serious, as it could cover the whole of DIS and have C Company completely pinned down. It was only 40 yards away, but we couldn't attack or fire on it effectively because of its position and the nature of the ground and we'd suffer many casualties if we withdrew. Harman went out alone, first crawling, before standing up and running at the machine gun bunker. The Japs saw him and fired continuously, but miraculously the bursts of fire went over his head. He reached the bunker entrance, pulled the pin from his grenade and let go of the clip. It only had a four-second fuse. He counted aloud and, as he said 'three', lobbed the grenade into the Jap position and dropped for cover. It exploded immediately. He then jumped to his feet, ran round into the bunker, checked the Japs were dead and returned to his position with the machine gun, to the cheers of the men.

By mid-morning the Japs had secured positions in the Fort north of the road junction to Kohima village and at the nearby Traffic Control Point (TCP). JIFFs (Japanese Indian Fighting Force) had occupied the village bazaar, and enemy artillery was positioned on outlying ridges, from where it could fire on part of the Garrison. Our own guns with the rest of 161 Brigade at Jotsoma couldn't reach them, so they had a free hand.

The Japs waited until dusk on the 8th before launching an infantry attack on DIS Spur, preceded by the usual mortar barrage. The weather was vile. The rain pelted down and made a hell of a racket on the metal roofs of the store *bashas*. Despite this, one ammunition

store was soon ablaze and lit up the surrounding area, so movement
was restricted. We didn't see the Japs forming up, but as they charged
they used grenade launchers, showering our positions with high
explosives and forcing us to keep our heads down as long as possible.
They didn't, however, get past our rifle and machine gun fire from
the weapon pits some 10 yards from the road. Bill Moxworthy was
in one with his crew, Corporal 'Taffy' Rees and two privates; Ted
Wells and Skingsley were in another; then came Privates Hankinson,
Hill and Cummings; next were Privates Allchin and Hills; and
Lawrence, Goodall and Naylor were in another further up the hill.
Below them were Corporal Webber and Privates Nobby Hall, Gunter,
Lehman and 'Butch' Tacon. They had four Brens and mowed the Japs
down in droves.

Despite the vastly superior numbers of the Japanese, no one
retreated. Men were killed in their trenches rather than fall back.
Dennis Cook, a lance corporal, was in one of C Company's forward
positions. The Japs were everywhere. He thought his number was up
but was fortunate enough to survive to tell his tale. Many others were
killed or wounded. We used everything to stop them, rifles, Brens,
grenades and bayonets in close-quarter hand-to-hand fighting on the
parapets of trenches. They didn't get past. What was apparently
soldiers of the Jap 58th Regiment tried to use ladders on the steep,
almost inaccessible slopes to the side of the road. Grenades were used
to repel them, but they kept trying. As we were forced back, the Japs
began to occupy some of our vacant trenches, making things very
difficult for our lads in the nearby positions. We eventually forced
them out, but not without further losses. The Japs mounted three
separate assaults on the hill, each with over two hundred more troops.
Our Brens got so hot that the barrels had to be repeatedly changed,
and ammunition was used so quickly that the supply to the guns was
difficult to maintain. As the Japs charged we fired and they fell like
ninepins. Their losses were horrendous but they didn't seem to be
bothered; they kept coming and we kept shooting.

C Company suffered many casualties, but they held out, the Japs
failing to take any ground whatsoever. D Company also suffered
badly, with men being killed and wounded. A mortar bomb exploded,
killing Corporal Albert 'Wally' Want and wounding Corporal Gilbert

in the leg. By now, 16 Platoon was reduced to three men. The attack lasted for nearly three hours, finishing about 10pm. An hour later, Naylor heard a jeep and went back to report it. As he came up the hill Private Lovell, thinking he was a Jap, shot him in the leg. Sergeant Tacon took him back to the ADS. The Japs were so close to our lines that C Company couldn't repair their trenches and any movement was virtually impossible. Eight Brens were arranged in a cross fire and, though no other improvements were possible, the ammunition supply to the forward trenches was better. This didn't seem to register with the Japs; they moved about freely, so we shot them. Tom Greatley watched in amazement as a Jap officer wandered up the road. He dropped his trousers and squatted down to relieve himself without any concern as to who could see him. Tom didn't allow him any privacy and shot him.

C Company were now exhausted through lack of sleep. Losses were high, and the defensive perimeter couldn't be properly manned. Most of the shrubs and small vegetation had disappeared under the enemy bombardment. The trees were heavily scarred and had lost their leaves where branches had been blasted away. Some were just spiked trunks now. Amazingly, little red and yellow finches came back and perched on the jagged remains. The enemy continued their regime of shelling at dawn and dusk. We called the latter 'Evening Hate'. They never let us down. They didn't discriminate in their targets either. Shells falling around the ADS killed nearly forty, most of them already wounded. The tree bursts did the most damage.

Snipers were getting amongst us. They were in the trees, hidden amongst the leaves that were left, where you couldn't see them, and they picked people off at will. Our own Company sniper was called Cousins. He was red hot. He bagged seventeen Japs in one day. On one occasion he must have shot a sniper in a tree twenty times. He thought he had missed and was losing his touch, until he realized the Jap was already dead. He'd tied himself to the tree so didn't fall out. Somehow a sniper had made it on to the hill and was positioned in a tree behind BHQ. He swept the area with automatic fire. Heffernan, the CO's batman, calmly took his rifle and got him with his first shot. He too was tied to the tree, his body hanging there for the rest of the siege.

There seemed to be no twilight. When darkness came it was all of a sudden. Well, it was pitch black on this night. There was no moonlight to help us out, and it was terrible for those in the front line trenches. They could hear the Japs shuffling about but could see almost nothing, only shapes and they couldn't be certain what these were. They could've been anything. Our eyes played tricks on us then, especially when we were that tired. If you fired, and it wasn't anything, it could give your position away or provoke an attack. It would at least lead to everyone standing to, so there would be no chance of any rest except for those lucky enough to have a comrade left alive and sharing the trench to keep lookout. During the night they attacked again, but this time it was different. They found out where our mortars were and concentrated their artillery on these positions, reducing the mortars' effect. The Jap infantry charges were now more difficult to resist, and they exploited this by gaining positions here and there. The usual barrage preceded the attacks, but they also used grenade launchers that gave the impression they were closer than they actually were. These launchers were hand-held, and they set them off in showers with devastating effect. They attacked the Deputy Commissioner's Bungalow area twice, first from the northern Fort area, secondly from the direction of the main road junction. They suffered massive losses but unfortunately for us managed to get small footholds on the Bungalow side of the road by the once immaculately maintained gardens. The beautiful rhododendrons and other flowers and shrubs had disappeared, and the bright red tiled roof was broken and smashed.

The Japs capitalized on their gains straight away, and reinforcements poured in as they prepared for the next attack. They even used one of our captured 3.7-inch guns against us. Some soldiers manned a Bren gun as they withdrew back to the Tennis Court terrace, where they were told to hold out to the last round. They did, and after a heroic stance that secured the withdrawal, they were overrun, bayoneted and shot. One chap pretended to be dead and had a very frightening time lying doggo as Japs walked and trampled over what they assumed to be his dead body. He couldn't make a sound or a movement. They'd have killed him if they'd found out. He managed to escape the next day by running back through mist to our lines. He was shot in the foot for his trouble by one of our men who mistook him for a Jap, but he was all right and gave us some very useful information about the Japs' strength and positions.

The Japs moved up to the chain-link fence on the east side of the Tennis Court. Some of A Company led by Sergeant Brooks were detailed to help the mixed units of troops already there. They dug in at the rear of the Deputy Commissioner's Bungalow, around the Tennis Court, about twenty yards from the enemy and around the Garrison Telephone Exchange. We could see the Japs digging in but dared not attack as we weren't ready and there were too many of them. Sergeant Brooks and his men dug in by the Clubhouse and Mound on the terrace to the rear, where a Bren was set up with a good field of fire. Lieutenant Hinton with his platoon dug in on the other flank, with Major Tom Kenyon and his men in between. Movement on the Tennis Court was restricted due to the two sides being so close to each other. Both we and the Japs used grenades. No one could move. We just had to wait. The Japs mounted a third attack of the night at IGH on some mixed troops from the convalescent depot and rest camp and forced them to withdraw despite strong resistance.

That evening, the Jap guns gave Summerhouse Hill a terrible pounding, the worst to date. All the shells seemed to be directed at my trench. At the same time the Japs attacked C Company from Jail Hill. Again it was with wave after wave of fanatical, screaming troops. It was the heaviest attack so far. We cut them to ribbons but they kept coming. They lost hundreds but it didn't deter them, they didn't seem to care. Eventually, they were driven back, but we'd lost some ground. We could have done with some barbed wire to make defensive entanglements. That would've slowed them down, but there was none to be had.

Around midnight we heard Japs digging in. A couple of hours later, an enemy mortar opened fire. Its rapid fire rained shells on us. This was the worst mortaring to date, especially in the forward trenches, which took a hell of a battering. One shell landed in a weapon pit, killing Lieutenant Phythian's batman, Bob Walters. He took the brunt of the blast, falling on to his superior officer. This saved Phythian's life, although he received minor leg wounds. The Japs attacked after the barrage, but with the aid of the Indian guns on Jotsoma Ridge they were repelled and again suffered great losses.

Unfortunately, one of the Indian guns put a shell into the weapon pit occupied by Corporal 'Taffy' Rees and two privates, Wells and Skingsley. Ted Wells was killed, Rees and Skingsley were buried but managed to dig themselves out and moved to an adjacent trench.

The Jap infantry attacked again with two hundred men and again they were mown down. They used grenade launchers and two landed in a Bren gun pit causing it to collapse and killing the gunner, Allchin. It was so difficult see them in the darkness and pouring rain. Despite their casualties, the enemy were making some headway because of our lack of firepower from the trenches. There was some hideous hand-to-hand fighting. C Company was in a precarious position as Jail Hill was swarming with Japs and their snipers were picking our men off. They could clearly see many of our positions and it was impossible to put your head over the parapet of the trench in daylight without fear of having it blown off. Men got hit and there was no way to help them; they were just left to die. Something needed to be done quickly.

The Japs attacked DIS Spur again. The front line only extended 20 yards. We couldn't improve our defences because the Japs on Jail Hill fired at anything that moved. Roy Wellings had a near miss when some shrapnel from one of the shells passed across his back and through his clothing. It even cut through the supply of toilet paper that he kept tucked down his shirt, but he didn't get so much as a scratch on him. He told me later, 'The trouble being an infantryman is that you survive one battle only to go on and fight the next. The feeling of invincibility begins to wear thin.' He was right. How we got through it, I don't know.

After the initial barrage, the Japs ran up the hill screaming and shouting. Sergeant King's mortars helped take some out. They were very accurate and must have killed dozens, but the Japs still kept coming. There were so many of them. When they got within range the Brens and rifles opened up, cutting them down in droves, but some got through, finally being shot a yard or two from the Bren gun positions. Despite their horrific losses the Japs attacked again and again and managed to take some of the forward trenches. No one retreated. They fought until they were killed. The Japs were then only 25 yards from C Company's second line.

Tom Greatley was only eighteen then. (He'd joined up when he was sixteen. He was a big kid and looked a lot older. He went to the local police station, where they asked his age and he told them he was eighteen. He thought he would be found out when he reported to the barracks, but no one said anything, and that was that). He was with two other privates, Lockyer and Lewis, in a bunker with a vertical drop of about 12 feet to the adjacent road below. Tom was on guard while the others tried to get what rest they could. He was priming and fusing his grenades when he heard noises on the road below. He woke up his mates and had a look to see what was going on. The Japs had crept up with muffled weapons, wearing plimsolls so they wouldn't be heard. They had put a bamboo ladder up against the side of the bunker and started to make their way up when Tom took his grenades and dropped them over the side, killing them.

9 APRIL

That 9 April was Easter Sunday. No Easter eggs for us. It wasn't very happy either, raining and cold. Our Padre held the Easter Sunday service in the ADS. Only twelve attended. We tried to clear the Japs off IGH Spur, but although we pushed them back they still held on to some positions. Some troops from A Company counter-attacked those at the Bungalow area but couldn't shift them. Later that day, the rest of A company were sent down to the Bungalow area to dig in and reinforce the defences.

Our situation was getting worse, especially with the shortage of medical supplies and water. We were rationed to three quarters of a pint a day. That was too little in those conditions, and thirst became a big problem. Men tried to collect water during the incessant, pelting rain, using their helmets, dixies or anything else that would do the trick. Any amount collected would help alleviate what was now a constant thirst, but it was never enough. The enemy had already cut off most of the water some days ago and it was only available from a few places such as small streams or a joint on the mains water pipe. These were all under the noses of the Japs and could only be used at night. Les Crouch, another of the Pioneers, was positioned on the south slope of Summerhouse Hill at that time, behind the Deputy Commissioner's Bungalow. He spent most of his time on guard duty or collecting water, going on sorties to the remote water points two or three times a night. If he wasn't doing this he was reinforcing rifle companies that were short of men

The growing number of wounded was exhausting the medical supplies. The previous night, John Young, the MO, went out with some Indian sappers to the 53 IGH area and to our lorries to collect blankets and any medicines that were available. They were very brave going out amongst the enemy, but encountered no Japs and brought back what they could. Evacuation of the wounded wasn't an option and so the shallow crawl trenches were extended. The doctors did what they could with the limited facilities available, but it was terrible when, after they had patched patients up, they were wounded again or even killed by enemy shells as they lay helpless in the crawl trenches.

On DIS Spur, C Company had cold mutton and biscuits for breakfast. That's all they had. During the early morning two Jap snipers were firing from Jail Hill and shot one of the sergeants, Arthur Crathern, who shared a forward trench with Roy Wellings. Corporal Norman fired smoke bombs so that the stretcher-bearers could get to him, but he was dead by the time they got him to the ADS. A twenty-two-year-old Brummie, Fred 'Nobby' Hall, was also hit in the head. They got him back into Corporal Norman's weapon pit, but the medics couldn't get to him without being hit themselves. He died after a few hours. You couldn't do much about it. The Japs were covering the area with a machine gun and cut down anything that moved. You didn't know where the enemy were and just kept your head down.

Donald Easten had already brought up some men to assist C Company and among these was John Harman. Just after first light, Easten noticed that the Japs were reworking one of C Company's old trenches, converting it to a machine gun pit to fire on our troops. Harman decided to attack it himself. He ordered his Bren gunner to cover him, moved out of his trench and ran down the hill through the trees towards the machine gun nest, ignoring the little cover available. Alec Haughton, another private in 'D' Company, saw him go and used his Bren to give supporting fire from further up the hill. Harman moved from side to side searching for the best position to overlook the enemy. The Japs shot back at him wildly. He stopped a few yards in front of their position and, firing his rifle from the hip, shot four of them before jumping into the weapon pit, bayoneting the fifth and making sure the others were dead. He reappeared holding the machine gun aloft and smashed it into the ground in front of everybody. Cheers went up from the surrounding soldiers at such a heroic deed, but John simply climbed up the ridge and walked back, despite shouts from his comrades to run. Just before he reached safety a Japanese machine gun from Jail Hill shot him in the lower spine. Easten ran out and pulled him back. He refused treatment and died a few minutes later. For this and previous actions he was posthumously awarded the Victoria Cross.

Corporal Trevor 'Taffy' Rees had stood up to watch Harman from the edge of his weapon pit. He didn't realize that the Japs had fixed-line machine guns on that pit and he was hit, falling into a dip a couple of yards away. Sergeant Tacon tried to recover him, was shot in the arm and the leg for his trouble, but managed to roll back into his position. Poor Rees was paralysed and no one could help him. He became delirious, screaming in pain, praying aloud and calling for his mom and dad. Tom Coath tried to set up a smokescreen so that the stretcher-bearers could get to him, but it was no good; the Japs knew what we were up to and saturated the area with fire. It took eight hours for him to die. It was an awful way to go and upset everyone.

The Peacock brothers were in trenches fairly close to each other. Private Peacock manned a Bren gun. His brother, a Lance Sergeant in D Company, was alone in his trench, his trench mate having been killed during a mortar barrage. During a quieter moment he dropped off to sleep through sheer fatigue. When he came round he found he was sharing his trench with a Jap officer. He couldn't find his rifle and had to fight the man with his bare hands. After a fierce struggle in the small trench he broke the Jap's neck, then ran him through with his sword to make sure

The Japs attacked the Tennis Court at 10 in the evening, preceded by the usual artillery and mortar bombardment. You couldn't see much from A Company's position because of steep slopes, so we didn't see them form up on the lower terrace. We could hear them, though, with their screeching and yelling, so we knew they were coming. Contact was made with Major Yeo's 24th Mountain Battery guns outside the perimeter at Jotsoma and with the mortars of RWK's Sergeant King. They let them have it, with very accurate fire to within 20 yards of 'A' Company's lines. Not one of our lads was hit. Despite this the enemy were still able to initiate an infantry charge and get through to A Company's lines. We couldn't see them coming in the darkness and mist, but silhouettes and shapes suddenly appeared in front of us. There was no time to pick your target, there were too many of them. We used grenades, and the Brens swept the area. That did the trick. The attack only lasted half an hour but A Company suffered losses and reserves were called in.

During the battle A Company's CSM went to collect some grenades from alongside one of the *bashas*. He heard voices inside and continued with the job in hand until he realized they were Japs. He immediately fetched a section of men and, armed with a tommy gun and grenades, cleared the hut, killing those inside. The Japs continued to attack through the night at various positions trying to penetrate A Company's line. It was pitch black, and what with the pouring rain and noise of battle it was impossible for Major Tom Kenyon in charge of A Company to know what was going on. The Japs seemed to be everywhere. Sergeant Brooks and his men were under a great deal of pressure from Jap attacks by the Clubhouse. We threw grenade after grenade down the slope at the enemy on the terrace below, and those remaining were cut down by Bren and rifle fire.

Corporal Ted Culmer was there. He had two brothers in the battalion, Wally and Tom. Wally was also at Kohima; Tom, fortunately for him, was left behind. Ted was a dispatch rider but there was no need for that here. He was now manning a Bren, pointing it towards the Jap lines. When thunder and lightning started, so did the Japs. They sent over their mortar barrage followed by an infantry charge, at the same time showering the positions with grenades. Culmer emptied magazine after magazine into them, his private changing them as they ran out. The Japs got to the edge of A Company trenches, where they hesitated, undecided where to run next. Culmer and the others mowed them down until there were none left. The second wave followed shortly after, but although by this time Yeo's mortars had reduced their numbers, there were still too

Ray Street (far left) with brother and family, late 1930s.

Ray Street in Lucknow, 1944.

Norton Barracks.

Tom Hogg.

(L to R) John 'Tops' Topham, John Laverty, Peter Franklin and Douglas Short.

'The Tunnels' through the Mayu mountains.

George Martin's grave.

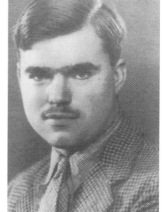

John Harman VC.

John Laverty and Douglas Short take a break on the Tiddim Road.

17

Kohima before the siege – the Deputy Commissioner's bungalow.

The bungalow gardens, before the siege.

The ruins of the bungalow after the siege.

The battlefield of Kohima after the siege.

The Imphal road, from a bunker on DIS.

Lorries on the Imphal road.

Kohima – after the battle.

Repairs to the track near Jessami.

The ruins of the bungalow, from the tennis court.

Graves on the Kohima battlefield marked for later identification

Gordon Inglis.

Padre Randolph.

Corporal Veall.

Jack Eves.

*Douglas Short,
John Steddy,
Donald Easten,
Tom Kenyon.*

*Front row: Tom
Coath, 'Tops'
Topham, Fred
Collett*

Jack Faulkner.

Victor King.

Ernie Stonnel and Ivan Daunt carving names on the Kohima Cross.

Ted Culmer.

Colonel Laverty receiving the DSO from Admiral Lord Louis Mountbatten.

Simla, looking towards Jakho, 1944.

Firpo's Restaurant, Chowringee, Calcutta.

Ray Street in Simla, 1944.

HQ at Milestone 143 on the Tiddim road.

Chin villagers preparing for a feast

The 161st Brigade Memorial at Kohima, December 1944.

Memorial service, December 1944.

The Kohima Cross, erected December 1944.

John Harman's grave, December 1944.

Royal West Kents visit graves at the tennis court, December 1944.

Shwedagon Pagoda, Rangoon, 1945.

WHEN YOU GO HOME
TELL THEM OF US AND SAY
FOR YOUR TOMORROW
WE GAVE OUR TODAY

Memorial erected in Kohima to those who died in the Siege.

Kohima at peace, photographed by Tom Hogg, December 1944.

many of them. Again, Culmer and the others fired. Sergeant Brooks brought him more ammunition as he was using so much. By now the Bren barrel was too hot, and his private had been wounded in the chest and lay at the bottom of the trench, so he had to change it himself, hoping that the Japs wouldn't get him during the break in firing. They didn't, and he continued replacing the magazines until it all went quiet. Despite the enemy pressure all their attacks were successfully thwarted and A Company had held on – just. The action of the day caused further losses amongst us: Lance Corporal Sam King and Corporal Reg Bowles copped it, as did Privates Reg Cook and Godfrey Stenner.

Another attack that night was directed on the Assam Rifles' position on IGH Spur. The Japs undertook probing attacks to assess the strength of their defence. The next morning the dead Japs were identified as part of the 138th Regiment of the 31st Japanese Division. We already knew we were up against the 124th Regiment and now, with this evidence, we now became aware that the enemy could number up to 15,000 men. We, on the other hand, at the beginning of the siege had only 1,500 combatants at most. Things were looking distinctly bad.

Chapter 5

The Siege of Kohima II
10–14 April 1944

10 APRIL

In the early light of 10 April C Company watched in despair as the Japs moved forward into vacated front line trenches. They removed the bodies of the dead men, theirs and ours, poured petrol over them and set them alight. We then watched our comrades burn. The stench of burning flesh was terrible and upsetting. It was wet and misty after the storm the previous night, and both C and D Companies were desperately short of men. They hadn't been at full strength at the start of the siege. A and B Companies weren't that bad, but were not at full strength either. B Company had never replenished its numbers after involvement in the earlier actions in the Arakan in Burma. C Company had now suffered over fifty per cent casualties, and with the Japs occupying the company's forward trenches their position was far from secure. Reinforcements were needed urgently or they would be overrun. Later that morning, Laverty sent reinforcements from HQ Company. C Company were ordered to hold on for the rest of the day and withdraw to FSD (Field Supply Depot) Hill that evening.

Whilst awaiting the order to withdraw, C Company busied themselves booby-trapping the approaches to DIS Spur and FSD Spur and destroying the plentiful supplies of food and stores so that they would not fall into the Japs' hands. Vehicles and equipment were pushed into the *nullahs*. Tom Greatley, a private in C Company, punctured the tins of fruit so they would go off in the heat, drinking some of the juice to quench his thirst. Apparently, tons of bully beef and fruit tins were destroyed this way. We couldn't take them with us, but we had to make sure the Japs couldn't get their hands on them. On one occasion Tom asked a chap in a nearby trench for some food. He obliged by throwing a can of soya link sausages to Tom which caught him in the face. Tom asked him whose side he was on.

We were in a terrible state by now, soaking wet and exhausted by constant battle readiness and lack of sleep. We had stopped washing and shaving days previously and we all sported beards. Our hair was getting longer and we stank. The atmosphere, made even worse by the smell of death and battle, was disgusting. The parapet to our trench smelled like a urinal. However, we were lucky as we could use a redundant shell hole to do our business, something they couldn't in the front line. They had to relieve themselves in the trench, and there was not much room to manoeuvre there. Tom Greatley told me that his mate would turn the other way whilst he did 'the necessary' into one of the old SEAC (South East Asia Command) magazines. He would then wrap the contents up and throw them as far as he could towards the Jap lines. He didn't know if he hit anyone because he couldn't keep his head up that long.

Battle fatigue wasn't a problem for the Japs. They sent in fresh troops every time, so it didn't affect them. It was different for us, because we couldn't rest. There was the continual threat of snipers and sporadic gunfire. It meant food was difficult to distribute from the cookhouse and it was almost impossible to get it to the front line; they had to do with bully beef and biscuits. But food wasn't the main concern. It was more important for the men to have effective weapons, and water to quench their now desperate thirst. They constantly cleaned their rifles and Bren guns so they wouldn't jam when under attack, particularly the Brens as they were such important weapons. We would've been lost without them and the grenades. This daily regime helped take our minds off the constant craving for water and keep us alert so we wouldn't drift off to sleep.

'Tokyo Rose', the Jap propaganda unit, sometimes taunted us. They used some sort of loudspeaker, claiming our own main army had deserted us and left us to be killed. They tried to get the garrison to surrender their arms in exchange for good treatment. We would all go quiet for a moment – then the Brens opened up so they knew we still meant business. There was no way we would surrender. We'd heard rumours of the atrocious treatment the Japs elsewhere gave to those they'd captured. Surrender was a disgrace to them and they treated their captives with barbaric contempt, often torturing them before wrapping them in barbed wire and tying them to a tree for bayonet practice. That happened to one of our lads called Sinclair who was captured at Kohima.

About midday Corporal Norman and Privates Hankinson, Lovell, Thrussler, Johnson and Goodall were detailed to go forward to a position close to the Jap lines, with orders to hold their positions until C and D Companies withdrew back to FSD (Field Supply Depot) Ridge. It was a horrible job, suicidal to my mind. They were in a desperate state, exhausted and soaking wet, but they didn't complain. They must have had some bottle. They all deserved medals. They went right forward into an area where they were surrounded, only about 10 yards from the Japs. Their action helped give us time to lay booby-traps, destroy food supplies and burn the remaining *bashas*. They held their position for nearly six hours before they pulled back, virtually crawling all the way. Hankinson was wounded in the back later that night during the shelling of FSD Hill. Our withdrawal during that evening wasn't easy. The Japs on Jail Hill sent over sporadic mortar fire but really let us have it at dusk. The snipers were always waiting to catch us off guard. Lieutenant Phythian and B Company officer Gordon Inglis were hit by snipers. Inglis was detailed to get some ammunition from one of the *bashas*, but was hit in the head. He was a good soldier, very brave. He died three weeks later.

During the evening, C Company withdrew under constant mortaring by the enemy. Easten was shouting orders to Sergeant Boxwell when a mortar shell caught them. It blew Boxwell up, severely wounding him. Easten was thrown into a trench by the blast, his back dislocated and an arm wounded. He was taken to the ADS. Captain Fred Collett took over from Easten. C Company had further casualties: Privates Stan Weeks, Gerry Bloomfield, Cliff 'Ernie' Foord and John Haslam were killed in the hand-to-hand fighting that day, trying to repel an attack on a *basha* that the Japs took over in the evening. C Company was no longer a viable unit because of its losses, so joined up with D Company. Tom Coath took command. A Company wasn't in any better condition. If it hadn't been for their effective head cover they would have suffered horrendous casualties and would never have been able to hold their line. On several occasions the forward trenches ran out of ammunition, but Sergeant Williams repeatedly ferried boxes of grenades to the front line despite the terrific enemy fire and also helped reorganize the positions. He got the MM (Military Medal) for that. He was very brave. They all were.

Two older soldiers manned a Bren dug in on the Mound near the Clubhouse. We didn't know who they were. They weren't West Kents. They were from the odds and sods. They did a brilliant job, though. Their accurate fire cut the Japs to pieces as they attacked in wave after wave across the Tennis Court below them. I don't know how many they killed, but the Japs lost a huge number of men. The Japs realized what was going on, aimed their fire at the mound and one Bren gunner was killed. The other remained in position and manned the gun on his own until a mortar bomb got him as well.

Intermittent shellfire rained down on A Company most of the day, shaking the bunkers and weapon pits, temporarily blinding and choking the men inside with dust and smoke. Men were killed or badly wounded, and most of those that remained were shell-shocked, such was the intensity of the barrages. After each one, bent and splintered weapons were replaced and the defensive positions checked and repaired; then the men stood up and prepared for the expected infantry charge. But it didn't come. The line had held firm again.

Dennis 'Bill' Wykes, in A Company, was in a trench by the Tennis Court with a young Welsh lad called Williams. Wykes was desperate for something to eat (he always was), so much so that after one of the barrages he decided to run back in an attempt to get some biscuits. He jumped out of his trench and made about 10 yards before the next shell exploded. It had hit a tree four feet off the ground, and the blast threw him to the ground. He looked up, saw the smoke from the shell and scrambled hell for leather back into his slit trench, tumbling in head first. To his horror, he saw that the young Welsh lad had been hit in the stomach by a piece of shrapnel. His insides were hanging out. The lad grabbed Bill's hand and begged him not to let him die. Bill comforted him as best he could, called for the medics, and they took him to the ADS. He didn't make it. To this day, Bill Wykes doesn't know what made him run from his trench at that particular moment. He would probably also have been killed if he hadn't.

The Japs put down over one hundred mortar bombs in ten minutes around BHQ and the ADS that evening, killing and wounding many of those already injured. The stench was unbearable as men lay in their own excreta and urine. There were no bedpans. The persistent rain had washed away the soil, and parts of dead bodies were sticking out of their shallow graves, some black and in varying states of decay. Clouds of flies congregated around the dead and wounded, settling on men's wounds and creating further infection. The rain was getting into the shallow trenches where the wounded were lying on liquid mud. The numbers of casualties were increasing all the time at the ADS. The Indians even gave up some of their rations so the wounded could have a little more.

In the operating pits Young and his doctors worked incessantly, with hardly any rest. (They'd see over six hundred cases by the end of the Siege). What rest they got was taken fully clothed in any space they could find. Most of the time they snatched an hour or so here and there, then it was back to work. They worked in primitive conditions, and amputations were done with knives – mind you, their overuse made them blunt, more like hacksaw blades. They must have been under a terrific amount of stress, with shells falling all around. They had to treat all types of injury, including wounded men who were hit again or whose wounds became infected. They never complained. One doctor called Glover was shot on two separate occasions by snipers, only to be patched up and carry on. Even the wounded mucked in where they could, helping each other and giving words of comfort to those in a worse condition.

Major Shaw, who was wounded earlier in the siege, was inspirational despite the pain he must have suffered. He was always asking about what was going on at the front. He tried to pass the time by reading Shakespeare while trapped in his trench but couldn't concentrate on it. Then Padre Randolph lent him a Bible, and he found that easier and simpler to read.

Corporal Arthur Hay was a stretcher-bearer and always in the thick of it. He'd already won the Military Medal in the Arakan for tending to the wounded under heavy fire. It was the same at Kohima. He could never guarantee that he would get back when called upon to treat the wounded. One night, Privates Wheeler and Guildford went out with a stretcher to bring someone in. When they didn't return after ten minutes Hay went out to see what was happening. He didn't want to. He was overcome with malaria but had to go – there was nobody else. As he reached the forward dugouts he found the stretcher. Guildford was dead and Wheeler was nowhere to be seen, so he went back to his dugout and the malaria finally took hold. The next thing he remembered was two soldiers grabbing him under the arms and carrying him off the hill when we were relieved.

The situation was becoming dire. Our casualties were mounting: James Bradstreet, a Welsh lad called Dave Bunnell, Ivor Gwilt, Derrick Windle and Cecil Roberson were all dead. None of them was older than twenty-one. Lance Corporal George Mann and Private Don Oliver were killed as well. Would it be our turn next? These and other dark thoughts would come and go, especially on the long nights of guard duty. There would be thoughts of food and water, thoughts of home and the probability that we would never see it again. We had that feeling of not being in charge of our lives, like condemned men. But we couldn't run away. No one was going to take our place or do our job for us. Fate had decided we were going to fight in this battle and all of us had been picked for this time. Every man on this hill had been selected by fate and some, maybe all, would die. I thought a lot about home or going on leave, about eggs and chips, but most of all about water. I was desperate for something to drink. I went across to the cooks and asked for water. Colour Sergeant Jack Eves filled my mug but told me not to ask again. They needed all they had for cooking. I felt mean for asking, because the cooks kept us fed: a meal in the morning and another in the evening. The poor sods in the front line had nobody to ask.

I think everyone prayed at some stage. I did. It was all we had left sometimes. Trapped in my trench, I would read a strip of paper with prayers and the words of St John: 'Let not your heart be troubled neither let it be afraid.' I read it over and over again. This piece of paper had been given to me in a church canteen in England some eighteen months before, although at the time it seemed more like a hundred years earlier. Those eighteen months had passed very quickly, and I had been in action for only four of them. It seemed funny that eighteen months of your life could pass so fast yet the beginning of them could seem such a long time ago.

It was during this time that a bit of a mystery man appeared around BHQ. He was a lean, clean-cut type, English-speaking but with no visible rank and dressed like us in jungle green. I thought he might have been the Deputy Commissioner, Charles Pawsey, or the Garrison Commanding Officer, Colonel Hugh Richards, but never knew for sure. He was a kind chap and moved around the hill lifting our spirits as he moved between our trenches and BHQ. He stopped and talked to us, assuring us that relief would get through and telling us not to worry too much. We never knew who he was or where he came from and thought perhaps he was one of the 'odds and sods' from the early defence units. He seemed without fear of bullets and shells as he strolled along in the open as if defying the enemy. We never saw him again. The funny part about it was that no one ever brought him up in conversation either. But I would remember this man for ever, as he always had a smile and a friendly nod and was one of the few morale-boosters for us troops in the trenches.

On the night of the 10th one of the forward A Company positions received a direct hit. Sergeant Bennett immediately led some men forward under heavy enemy fire to replenish the positions, and they held off the frequent Jap attacks until relieved. The Japs continued to attack during the nights of the 10th and 11th, concentrating on FSD hill, to where C Company had fallen back, and around the Deputy Commissioner's Bungalow, where A Company was. Showers of grenades were launched before their infantry were sent forward yelling and screeching. A Company took the brunt of it but gave nothing away. The attacks were so fierce that one Scottish private picked up three automatic weapons from dead colleagues and emptied each one in turn into the oncoming Japs. There was no time to reload. After that he hurled his grenades before resorting to hand-to-hand fighting. At dawn, the Japs sent over a particularly heavy mortar barrage, during which we took further losses. Amongst these, Captain John Topham was wounded. My trench mate Ron Clayton was his batman and runner; he got on well with his officer and the news of his wounding upset him a great deal. Topham was the Signals Officer, a nice, kind, happy person, who used to come on some of the runs with me. We would often go out with a roll of thin telephone wire and lay new or dummy runs of cable or repair those damaged. Poor Topham was wounded again at the end of the siege when a shell exploded nearby as they were putting him on to one of the lorries. He died in hospital later.

Jack Faulkner was in his bunker, sitting with one hand on the phone, the other holding a cigarette on which he 'dragged' continuously. He thought of his girlfriend to try to take his mind off things; two other officers played cards for the same reason. Another had broken down and started crying. It was the pressure; you couldn't blame him. Then the shelling started and all hell was let loose. Shells fell all about them, one landing directly on the bunker roof. It didn't collapse, but sagged under the blast. The bunker filled with dust, and as it settled Sergeant Deacon came in. Men had been killed or wounded and there was a gap in the front line. Without saying anything, a resting wounded man and a shell-shocked soldier followed him out to go and plug the gap.

11 APRIL
This was a relatively quieter day. The Japs still attacked and sent over their shells, but it wasn't as intense as previously. We were still stuck in our trenches. We couldn't go anywhere. Ron Clayton had Topham's pack and took it to the signals bunker. He was told look after it in our trench until the action was over. That was a pain, as we didn't really have the room. In the pack were several paperback books and I demanded to have one. It would have been great to have something to read to take my mind off the battle, but Ron refused. They were his officer's property and not his to loan. I felt very angry, but he was adamant and wouldn't part with any, so that was that. I was too thirsty to argue and although annoyed, I respected his loyalty.

Trapped in our trench, Ron and I would talk about which way would be the best to escape if it came to every man for himself. We would look at the mountain range and devise a make-believe plan, knowing full well that we would have to fight hand-to-hand to get there. We would also talk of the leave we would get and what we would do when we got to Chowringee in Calcutta. Perhaps we would go to Firpo's, a well known restaurant. Everyone went there. We would order duck with green peas and potatoes, washed down with ice-cold beer. That was our dream. We talked of the many other places we would visit and of days and nights out. Maybe we would have a night out at an air-conditioned cinema. But first we had to get out of this siege, and the odds were distinctly against us.

At Kohima, we didn't really have any idea of dates and times. The passing of time was marked by the food we received; we got a meal in the morning and a meal at night. We would talk of home to try and take our minds off the situation we were in, but our thoughts soon turned to water and the chances of getting any from the cooks in the long trench nearby. The cooks allowed us to fill our mugs once more, then warned us not to ask again because the water was for cooking. We took the hint and never did but were still thankful for our extra ration. They did a cracking job keeping us fed in such conditions. Just because they were cooks, don't think they weren't brave. They were, incredibly so. Colour Sergeant Jack Eves was seen several times manoeuvring his large six-foot-four-inch frame from trench to trench, bringing warm food and tea to the front line. He appeared to show little concern for enemy snipers or shellfire. It was actions like his that lifted morale and made us more determined to hold on despite the odds. He didn't only deliver the food, he was in the action too. On one occasion he was by the DC's Bungalow and heard noises in one of the *bashas* nearby. It was some Japs smoking and talking. Jack and another sergeant threw some grenades in and killed them.

On FSD, C Company men had their first cooked breakfast since they arrived, but not all of them had withdrawn there. Due to the battle conditions some men had become isolated or hadn't heard the order. Tom Greatley was in a weapon pit on DIS Spur with Privates Lockyer and Lewis. He fell asleep through fatigue. When he woke up he heard talking above the head cover of the pit, and the language was Japanese. It was a hell of a shock. He was so scared he couldn't speak. That was just as well. He had to lie low until they moved on. When the coast appeared to be clear he jumped up, picking up his Bren and bandoliers of ammunition, and ran for his life towards FSD. He didn't know if he would make it or whether the Japs could see him. He didn't dare look back but kept going, fearing all the time he would be shot in the back. His helmet fell off as he ran, but he didn't bother picking it up. Running as fast as he could, he approached a large shell crater. He felt he didn't have time to negotiate clambering in and out of it, so jumped right across, Bren and all. To this day he doesn't know how he did it; it was a hell of a distance, but he did it and made it to the relative safety of his own lines. He didn't know what happened to the others; he never saw them again. At the same time, Roy Wellings was also still on DIS Spur with Corporal Joe Dent. Wellings had acquired a Bren, the gunner Crosbie having been wounded (he died later). They too had to bide their time before joining the others.

Three men came down from the command post and stopped by our trench for a chat and a smoke. They were in no hurry to go and do the dangerous job that they had been detailed for, getting rid of a machine gun post at DIS Spur by the road somewhere near the front line. Their talk was light, about getting some leave in India, but their thoughts were clearly not. They wanted the cigarettes to last forever. Their future was uncertain. I felt sad as they left and wished them good luck, feeling thankful that it wasn't us. Some time later, one of them returned, badly wounded, supported by two soldiers from a forward trench. When asked about the others, he shook his head and tears filled his eyes.

After dark, B Company led by Major John Winstanley took over A Company's positions around the Deputy Commissioner's Bungalow, with A Company dropping back to Kuki Piquet. Sergeant King and his mortar platoon took a position to the right by the Clubhouse and the Mound, Tom Hogg took his platoon to the centre and Sergeant Glyn Williams went to the left, where the land fell away steeply. Winstanley was a medical student before the war and returned home to become a prominent eye surgeon. He'd won a Military Cross in the Arakan. As soon as he and his men had settled in the Japs attacked. Winstanley had heard them forming up and asked for artillery back-up. He got it from Hill's 24th Mountain Battery and Sergeant King's mortars. Some Japs got through, only to be met by showers of grenades and the now familiar sound of the Brens that relentlessly cut them down.

A small Scottish private named Brown manned one of the Brens, with the rest of his section in support. He was a bit of a rough diamond, nothing special but a decent enough sort. He and his men were terrific and from their forward position controlled the Tennis Court. The enemy cottoned on to this and concentrated their fire on Brown's position, sending showers of grenades towards him. He didn't seem to care and stood up whilst firing the Bren to get a better field of fire. As members of his section were killed he continued firing relentlessly, shouting all the time for more ammunition and grenades. Eventually there was only him left, but he carried on loading and firing his gun and throwing grenades. He and his men must have shot hundreds, but the Japs got him in the end. Winstanley found him slumped over his Bren when he returned with some ammunition. Corporal Richards, a Welshman and ex-miner, took over from Brown and did a fantastic job holding out, only being relieved when the position had been made secure.

The Japs didn't seem to learn from their mistakes. Despite their losses they repeated their attacks in the same way. They always did. Twice more they attacked B Company that night and twice more they were repulsed with heavy casualties. The second and third attacks were heavier, with the aid of horrendous mortar fire and showers of hand-launched grenades. B Company's losses weren't light. The place was saturated with Japs, and they now held the area east of the Tennis Court as well as the area around the Bungalow. We still held the high ground and the positions around the Clubhouse, although the Japs managed to get snipers in some trees that overlooked the area. Several of Hogg's 10 Platoon were lost before we discovered where the Japs were firing from. Then some of the lads sorted them out. Due to the lack of tree and leaf cover the Jap snipers were having a field day. They didn't discriminate; they shot anyone who appeared within their sights, including non-combatants and the wounded. It must have been awful for the poor wounded in those shallow slit trenches, especially those who couldn't help themselves. There was hardly any cover, and chaps would see their comrade next to them shot, not knowing if they would be next.

Winstanley moved Hogg's platoon, or rather the eight men that were left in it, to the Clubhouse, where Tom Hogg set up three Bren guns. The Japs attacked both sides but the position was held. One Bren gun crew was lost, so Hogg had to man the position himself. In the early hours of the morning, under a full moon, Hogg heard Japs on the Tennis Court. It wasn't the usual screeching and wailing attack. They weren't wearing boots, just a type of plimsoll that disguised the sound of their advance. About a dozen of them rushed the position with fixed bayonets and one Jap charged at Hogg. Hogg tried to shoot him but couldn't get his shot off in time. The Jap drove his bayonet at him but fortunately for Hogg it got caught in his belt webbing, hardly injuring him at all. Hogg didn't mess about. He wasn't going to give the man a second chance and emptied the 25-round magazine into him. The main attack followed, with the Japs going through Hogg's positions, but fortunately Winstanley and his men to the rear sorted them out and the position held firm.

The next day, Hogg was in his position at the corner of the Tennis Court. Lance Corporal Hill, his only surviving NCO, asked if he could go with him should it come to every man for himself. Hogg of course agreed, but at that moment a grenade was lobbed into their trench. Hill turned his back on it and was severely wounded, but Hogg was unhurt. It took over a week for Hill to die. There were just three survivors of Hogg's 10 Platoon at the end of the Siege.

Despite this so-called 'quieter' day, our death toll still rose, not only as a result of the day's battle but because men were succumbing to earlier wounds, a situation exacerbated by the lack of basic medical facilities. It wasn't the medics' fault. They could only work with what they had. Nevertheless, the likeable Cockney barrow boy Corporal Bill Moxworthy, another Londoner, Fred Gipps, and Welsh lad Will Davies all died. Married men such as Charlie Sims, Privates Len 'Ginger' Fisher, Charlie Trussler and Gwilym Jones would never see their families again. Sergeant Les Peacock was finally parted from his twin brother. Derek Jack was also lost.

12 APRIL
At first light on 12 April the Japs attacked two platoons of our
supporting Rajputs on FSD hill. The Japs copped a right battering
and had to withdraw, leaving thirty of their dead strewn across the
hill. Our casualties weren't light, either. The ADS was now past
overflowing; men were moaning in the slit trenches for treatment or
something to relieve their pain. The medics were hopelessly short of
supplies and never seemed to stop to rest. Sergeant Gerry Boxwell
eventually succumbed to his horrific wounds and we heard that
Sergeant Harry Chantler and Private Eddie 'Tubby' Whittingham had
been killed. The water situation was becoming desperate and
ammunition was running low, especially grenades. We would have
been in trouble if they'd run out. Later, we had to give up some of
ours to supply the men by the Tennis Court, they were using so many.
Some men reckoned grenades were the best weapons at Kohima,
especially at night when you couldn't see the enemy to shoot;
moreover, they didn't give your position away like the flash or noise
from a rifle did. Tom Greatly heard that the Japs had got hold of some
of our grenades and were using them against us. They didn't go off
though, because they left the pins in. Our chaps gratefully threw them
back with the pins out!

It was thought that airdrops would do the trick. There wasn't any
alternative, as there was no other way to get supplies in, but even
airdrops would be difficult in that terrain. We had been pushed back
into an area no more than 500 by 500 yards, less than that in some
places. Every enemy shell seemed to kill or wound someone. There
were nearly 2,500 men in this area but fewer than 1,000 of them were
in action, the others being non-combatants or wounded. We were all
scared, the non-combatants even more so. They weren't used to
action. They used to huddle around BHQ not far from my trench.
Apparently, this was the safest area. I thought to myself that if this
was the safest place I couldn't imagine what it must be like in the
front line. One thing that did puzzle me about the non-combatants
was that, although some helped with the wounded or undertook other
tasks so that those in action could keep fighting, many just sat around
doing nothing. In fact, some refused to help, saying it wasn't their
duty. I thought that being in such a position they would have got hold

of a weapon and got stuck in, rather than waiting to die. But I didn't dwell on it all for too long. I had enough to concentrate on keeping myself alive.

Where we were, the Japs sent over their usual evening barrage. It was repetitive and worked its way as usual up Summerhouse Hill towards our position. (Earlier in the Siege we got down to the bottom of the trench straight away until the barrage was over, but as we got used to it we would watch the shells explode. It wasn't that we weren't scared. We were, but we were hardened now and sick of being stuck at the bottom of a hole). We watched as the Japs dropped mortars on those in front of us. When they got to a certain point we knew it would be our turn next and got down into the bottom of the trench. The first mortar bomb would explode about 25 yards or so in front of us, with a further six bombs slowly working their way up the slope towards our trench. They always came in sevens. We would count the explosions whilst lying low at the bottom of the trench; and after the seventh explosion we would jump up with our rifles cocked and bayonets fixed, ready for any attack by Japs that might have broken through our forward positions. We had done this for the last week. Fortunately, in our case, the immediate front line always held firm and the enemy never came.

We were lucky, though, as just forward of our position, troops were involved in hand-to-hand fighting with the onrushing Japanese. We could hear them after each barrage, the screaming and shouting of hundreds of Japs as they psyched themselves up for the forthcoming charge, followed by the shouts and screams of hand-to-hand combat. It was horrifying, as we never knew whether or not it would be our turn next. After the seventh mortar bomb exploded at the end of each barrage I would tense up, waiting to see if any Japs had broken through; this would be followed by the huge relief that our lads had held them off. I experienced this awful feeling every day at dawn and dusk.

This particular evening, number four mortar exploded on the rear of our trench. Clayton and I lay in the bottom of the trench and waited for the three more mortar bombs to come; we couldn't move until these had all exploded. A thick green smoke filled our trench, almost choking us. The explosion had blown dirt, pebbles and earth into the trench and on to our packs. A piece of shrapnel ripped open my pack and put a hole through my 1944 diary. Another piece cut through a bandolier of bullets, neatly slicing through a clip of ten .303s. How they failed to go off, I don't know, but we just counted our blessings that we were still alive. Clayton's blanket disappeared, presumably blasted elsewhere on the hill. We couldn't look for it anyway. For some reason Clayton had left his water bottle on the parapet of the trench. It was full of holes, leaving us with one water bottle to share between us. I wasn't at all pleased about that, as water was so scarce. We made sure we kept the remaining water bottle at the bottom of the trench after that.

Suddenly, the man in the next trench, a runner called Williams, panicked and started to get out of his trench. I don't know why. He just lost it. There was nowhere to go. Perhaps he thought he would run to the relative safety of the larger signals bunker, but there were three more mortars to come. He must have known that. The poor sod was blown straight back in as number five mortar bomb exploded in front of him. We immediately called for the stretcher-bearers, but they couldn't get him out; the trench was too narrow, so they had to leave him. It was awful for the poor chap. We couldn't risk tending to him for fear of being targeted ourselves, so he was left there until the next day, when things had quietened down and the medics came to take him to the ADS. When they arrived we had to thread a blanket around him, so that he could be lifted out in a sling-like fashion. Although badly injured he was well aware of what was happening, and we carried him back to the ADS. Unfortunately, although we got him to sickbay his injuries were so severe that he died three days later. He was married with kids and a good soldier, too. He'd served in the Middle East, seeing more action than most. He was a caring sort of chap. (It was he who had helped a shell-shocked runner who came out of a barrage by the Tunnels. The man didn't know where he was, but Williams grabbed him and helped sort him out). He also helped out with the wounded and would often take time out to talk to them. I just think it got to him in the end.

That night the Japs were as predictable as ever. They let us have their barrages, followed by wild infantry charges or 'jitter' patrols, on which they would creep up quietly to try to identify the best place to attack our positions. During one of the barrages, D Company Sergeant Major Haines got wounded and was instantly blinded. He didn't go to the ADS, though. He refused treatment and ordered a private to lead him around the front line continually barking orders at his men and giving encouragement to build up morale. It worked, too.

13 APRIL

Things reached an all-time low on 13 April. The Japs sent over a storm of shells and the ADS suffered two direct hits. It was awful. Over twenty men were killed, including two of the doctors we couldn't afford to lose; we didn't have enough medics to start with. Private Paddy Fall was in there being treated for tropical ulcers on his legs. He'd only just had his twenty-fourth birthday the day before. Stan Calton and Albert Hankinson, wounded in past actions, were also there. They were both killed. Privates John Brattman and nineteen-year-old Clem Keating were also lost. Many more of the injured were wounded a second time, crying out in pain. A head, limbs and other body parts littered the area. The ADS was completely wrecked.

Lieutenant Colonel John Young, the officer in charge, was also wounded but remained on duty and immediately made arrangements for the construction of a new ADS. Barrett's Indians and non-combatants, together with some of our lads, rebuilt the Dressing Station, which was operational by the afternoon. This time it was more sturdily constructed. It was six feet deep by ten feet long with four-foot trenches to access it. The roof was better, too. A mortar hit it shortly afterwards but no real damage was done. Unfortunately, a lot of important medical equipment had been lost and now there wasn't enough medicine or supplies to treat the wounded; men who should have survived were dying because of this. We now knew that however serious our wounds, we couldn't be guaranteed a safe bed. This began to affect the morale of the medics, seeing chaps die after they had their wounds treated because the after-care was insufficient. It affected everyone, really, as the medics were a great source of comfort and a boost to the morale of the men whether they were wounded or not.

Fred Worth, a mate of Bill Wykes, was a private in A Company and his position had been overrun. He got away with it but was shot in the foot whilst running back. The wound didn't seem too bad but he said he could 'feel something rattling about inside his boot'. He went to the ADS for treatment but didn't make it. Due to the poor conditions and lack of proper medical care he contracted gangrene and died three days later. It was horrible. You don't expect to die from a foot wound. A Welsh chap called Stenner was luckier. He got lost, had to run back and jumped into the first hole he could find. He didn't have time to think. Fortunately, it was behind our lines so he was safe. Unfortunately, it was the latrine. It wasn't pleasant, but better than the alternative.

The water containers in the ADS were punctured during the shelling and the supply lost. Airdrops were now critical. Lives depended on them. As if that wasn't bad enough, things now went from bad to worse. The first airdrops, when they actually started to take place, were a disaster. You couldn't blame the pilots. It wasn't their fault. The weather was terrible at times and the maps available were only to a very small scale. I don't suppose any better ones existed of such inhospitable terrain. The area we were in was so small it would have been hard to hit if it had been flat, let alone sited amongst jungle and mountains. A dropping zone was agreed and yellow strips were laid out in the shape of the letter 'T'. Indian non-combatants, who had cleared the area under constant sniper fire, did this.

Flares were used to guide the first Dakota aircraft in, but the pilot must have overshot and dropped the supplies behind the Jap lines. These included a mortar and ammunition that they used against us. Two other planes succeeded with their drops, but many of the parachutes landed in the trees, and with the Jap snipers about it was a dangerous business retrieving them. You could clearly see the small figures in the aircraft push the cargo out and the parachutes blossom, swaying in the wind as they fell. Water was dropped in petrol cans and we watched in despair as the Japs shot holes in them as they hung from the trees. Some of the water cans tore loose from their chutes and crashed into the ground, bursting on impact. The water quickly soaked into the dry ground as thirsty men helplessly looked on. Not all the 'chutes opened, and a couple of Indians were killed when one of the drops landed on them. Sergeant Bob Clinch and some others helped recover what they could from the airdrop. John Young recovered some of the medical supplies after dark, and medicines and painkillers were given to the wounded. This greatly improved the operation of the ADS. However, very little water was recovered and the situation was past desperate. Airdrops continued daily after that.

We had problems on FSD. The Japs were amongst D Company, and units of the Assam Rifles were sent in to sort the situation out. They did well but suffered heavy losses and pulled back. Unfortunately, the Japs could now fire directly into our trenches and we had to pull back. Since the Japs had taken DIS Spur they could overlook nearly all our positions on FSD, and with the absence of tree and leaf cover we were easy pickings. Our Rajputs were in a forward position and took a right pasting before men from A Company relieved them. They had lost their only British officer and this affected the men. Some were in tears. However, their Subedar (Captain) Sultan Singh, although very upset, rallied the men and got them back on track.

The rest of A Company came up from Kuki Piquet together with Tom Coath and the remainder of C Company, now reduced to fifteen men. Jap snipers had killed Sergeant Henry Norton and Corporal Harry Morley.

That night the Japs put in desperate attacks on A and D Companies on FSD hill, wearing plimsolls and carrying their weapons wrapped so we couldn't hear them. Lieutenant Doresa ordered his men to hold their fire until the enemy was within 15 yards. The Bren gunner, Private Peacock, was told not to fire until the Japs were only five yards away. This was very difficult as the area was saturated with Japs and their shadows were everywhere as they moved amongst the remaining tree and leaf cover. When the order to fire was given the whole platoon joined in and parachute flares lit up the area. A chap in D Company shot three Japs one by one as they jumped into his trench. A and D Companies lost a considerable number of men, but the Japs' losses were heavier still and they were forced to withdraw without any gain. These 'jitter' tactics weren't their regular approach. They nearly always made a right racket, shouting at us in English to give up before they charged. Of course, this gave us a chance to call

for artillery and mortar fire, which thinned them out before they got
to our Brens, rifles and grenades, and eventually to hand-to-hand
combat and bayonets.

The pressure was still intense by the Tennis Court. Bodies of the
Jap dead were strewn everywhere and the stench was awful. B
Company's losses were severe. When Sergeant Glyn Williams was
wounded in the neck and taken to the ADS, he didn't hang about.
Although partly paralysed down one side, he returned to his platoon.
There was no point in staying there. There was no space. Anyway,
all hands were needed in the front line. The men were exhausted and
this was beginning to have a serious effect: weapons were jamming
on a regular basis, because the men were so tired that they didn't, or
rather couldn't, keep them clean and dry.

Private Walter Williams and Corporal Veall were manning a
Bren on the Mound behind the Clubhouse when some Japs attacked.
The Bren jammed, and the enemy bayoneted Veall. Williams
thought he'd had it. He didn't have time to find a weapon but picked
up a shovel and ran at the Japs. He swung it, killing the first Jap
then going after the others. To his surprise, they ran off. More Japs
managed to break through and got into the Clubhouse. This was a
very dangerous situation. Victor King attacked them with grenades
and that got rid of them. Throughout the night the Japs attacked,
their assaults preceded by showers of hand-launched grenades.
Bitter battles took place, with the West Kents holding their fire until
the last possible moment, inflicting high casualties on the enemy.
Then it was down to hand-to-hand fighting and the bayonet, until
the Japs were repulsed again without any gain.

Gwynfryn Bennett, also in B Company, was in a trench by the
Deputy Commissioner's Bungalow at first. It had a corrugated metal
head cover which he held up using his rifle. When a shell landed close
by, it blew the cover away, also bending his rifle barrel and rendering
it useless. They had to move back to a trench to the rear, but needed
to look out for snipers. Although Bennett just made it, his trench mate
didn't; a sniper got him. Bennett spent the next few nights alone in
his trench so had to be on the alert all the time. He couldn't afford to
be caught off guard when the Japs came. When the Japs charged we
gave them everything, then it was down to hand-to-hand fighting and

bayonets. The bloke in the next trench was promoted to lance corporal for his bravery.

This day, 13 April, was the worst day of the Siege so far and became known as the 'Black Thirteenth'. Of the 446 officers and men of the Royal West Kent Regiment who had been deployed originally, 150 were now either dead or wounded. C Company had suffered so many losses that it was no longer a viable unit. Roy Wellings, who had become separated from C Company, remained with Sergeant Brooks and a platoon of A Company until the end of the Siege.

14 APRIL
During the actions on the night of the 13th/14th, Major Peter Franklin led a water party of Indian sepoys to a small spring near B Company's position. About twenty men used small canvas sacks called *chagals* to collect the water. It took ages to fill them, but over twenty gallons was collected in about five hours and shared between the Companies and ADS. It was most welcome and necessary.

About three in the morning, three men I thought were non-combatants appeared. Somehow they had got through our front line positions and now were standing several yards away from me. I ordered them to halt. They huddled together, none of them reached for any weapons, and I had my rifle levelled at them. They had no means of identification, so I was uncertain what to do. Apart from the Royal West Kents at Kohima there were hundreds of Asian troops. Many didn't have British steel helmets and some had incomplete or no British uniforms. So it was hard to say if someone unwashed and dressed in this or that was on our side or the enemy's. Many were unable to speak English, and the English of those that could was rather hit and miss. I was faced with a difficult decision: should I blast them away, only to find out I had killed or wounded three unarmed, innocent local tribesmen and caused the already exhausted troops to stand to unnecessarily – or should I let them pass? Also, what if the men in the front line positions heard someone apparently attacking BHQ? What would they do? Perhaps there might be other hidden enemy troops waiting for these three fall guys to take the fire, thus identifying our positions so they could attack in force. Confused, I hesitated, but eventually waved them through. They moved on, huddled together and looking back with frightened, strained faces as they continued up to the top of the hill, on to the track and out of sight. As I hadn't received a password from them, I should have shot them, but I just couldn't bring myself to do that.

I had learnt a lesson days before while on night guard. I heard action down by the Tennis Court in front of us, shouting and fighting. It appeared that the Japs had broken through and were making their way up and through to BHQ. I immediately grabbed one of my grenades and pulled the pin, getting ready to throw it at the oncoming enemy. But they didn't come, and when I had waited several minutes I realized that they had been held. So there I was, standing with this grenade ready to throw, the pin released and discarded on the ground somewhere. Of course, to throw the grenade would be wasting valuable ammunition and also would draw attention to our position. Therefore we had to look for the lost pin. I held the grenade in one hand and Clayton and I searched the bottom of the trench for it. After a few nerve-racking minutes, which seemed an age, Clayton found it. He gave it to me and I pushed it back into the grenade. Then I placed the grenade on the parapet in case of further attack and eventually drifted off to sleep. As dawn approached I awoke to see the grenade lying on the edge of the trench with its sprung arm straining to release itself. The split pin had been incorrectly housed, only half of the pin's stem being in the correct position, the other half having been bent out of shape. I immediately woke Clayton, went across to the parapet and withdrew the pin. Whilst holding the grenade handle steady, I straightened the pin with my teeth, made the grenade safe and put it back into my pack.

On 14 April, units of the Assam Rifles relieved B Company by the Tennis Court, and Winstanley's men pulled back to IGH Spur. They didn't complete this until almost dark because the enemy snipers were so accurate. We had an airdrop in the morning but sadly one of the planes crashed into GPT Ridge. We didn't know whether any of the airmen survived. We didn't like to think about it. It might have been better for them to be killed than fall into the hands of the Japs. During the rest of the day the Japs peppered the Garrison with mortar fire and high explosive rounds. Some of the wounded had recovered enough to return to their units, making room in the ADS for the less fortunate. Mind you, it wasn't safe in the ADS. Jap shells were always falling around it.

A forward patrol spotted four Japs chatting in a bunker on FSD hill. The Japs saw them too and beckoned them to come over. The patrol didn't know if they were going to surrender or trying to be friendly. Anyway, they couldn't take the chance, not with the Japs. The patrol leader went back to his Commanding Officer, Jack Faulkner, for orders. He had a look himself and sent the patrol back with a Bren and a section of men, who shot them.

It was misty that morning, and at about midday the Japs laid down smoke and attacked some positions occupied by various non-RWK men brought in to replace some of our casualties. There were forty of them and they attacked with gelignite and grenades as they tried to blow up our positions. Our men had to retreat up the hill as the Japs moved forward. However, our flanking troops peppered the area with mortars and small arms fire, halting the Jap advance and killing many as they withdrew. Around ten in the evening the Japs tried to infiltrate through A Company's positions on FSD hill. They couldn't see them properly. They were just shapes dodging amongst the trees. Some Japs got into one of the *bashas* close by. We couldn't let them stay there as they could overlook our positions, but we had a hell of a game getting them out. Jack Faulkner was sent to deal with it and went out armed with a Molotov cocktail (petrol bomb). He lit the fuse and threw it into the *basha*, but it didn't go off. Bullets and grenades weren't working, nor were the Molotov cocktails, so Jack Faulkner used more petrol, doused on the walls, followed by a grenade. That did the trick, setting the *basha* alight. Flames were everywhere. The Japs ran out, some only half dressed, and down the hill only to be caught by the waiting Bren gun manned by Private Ferguson. Again the effects of battle fatigue showed, as the gun jammed and most of the enemy escaped.

Lieutenant Johnson led a patrol of 4th/7th Rajputs from 161 Brigade at Jotsoma into our perimeter. God knows how they got through in one piece as the area was infested with Japs, but they did. Our Commanding Officer, Lieutenant Colonel Laverty, told Johnson that the RWKs' spirits were all right but that we were exhausted and there weren't enough of us to hold on much longer. He added that unless help came within forty-eight hours Kohima would fall. Johnson and his Rajputs left and took the message back to Jotsoma.

On this day, Colonel Hugh Richards, the Garrison Commander, issued an 'Order of the Day'. It read:

> I wish to acknowledge with pride the magnificent effort which has been made by all officers, NCOs and men and followers [non-combatants] of this Garrison in the successful defence of Kohima.
>
> By your efforts you have prevented the Japanese from attaining this objective. All attempts to overrun the Garrison have been frustrated by your determination and devotion to duty. Your efforts have been in accordance with the highest traditions of British arms.
>
> It seems clear that the enemy has been forced to draw off to meet the threat of the incoming relief force and this in itself has provided us with a measure of relief. His action is now directed to contain us by harassing fire, while he seeks to occupy odd posts under cover of that fire.
>
> The relief force is on its way and all that is necessary for the Garrison now is to stand firm, hold its fire and beat off any attempt to infiltrate among us.
>
> By your acts you have shown what you can do. Stand firm; deny him every inch of ground.
>
> I deplore the sufferings of the wounded: every effort is being made to alleviate them at the first opportunity.
>
> Put your trust in God and continue to hit the enemy hard wherever he may show himself. If you do that, his defeat is sure.
>
> I congratulate you on your magnificent effort and am confident that it will be sustained.
>
> Hugh Richards, Colonel
> Commander Kohima Garrison
> 14 April 1944

This order was typed out and handed round the troops under fire. It gave us a huge lift and the determination to believe we might just get out of this alive. But there was still plenty to do. Apart from those wounded, we lost fourteen more men killed that day. It was the worst death toll yet. Three Williamses were killed or succumbed to their wounds. Some of the other Welsh lads, Corporal Len Rees and Privates Steve Roberts and Ken Davies, were also lost. Among the others that died were Corporal Eddie Hatton and Privates George Fidler, George 'Sid' Baker, Charlie Gray, Percy Hughes, Don Mancey, Russell Gartrell and one of the Collins brothers , Len. Most had young wives, now widows.

Chapter 6

The Siege of Kohima III
15–20 April 1944

15 APRIL

This was a regular day: the enemy sticking rigidly to their methods and letting us have the usual artillery and mortar barrages. The heaviest barrage was concentrated on FSD Hill, inflicting more casualties on A and C Companies. We'd been told that relief was on its way but didn't take that much notice. That was old news that never seemed to materialize, although we hoped it would before it was too late. Apparently, Laverty was told that relief would come the next day and made arrangements for some of the wounded to be evacuated. I never heard any more about it, and the relief didn't come. We were stuck in our trench by BHQ. We couldn't go anywhere, not with the snipers about. We sat and talked, cleaned our weapons or tried to grab some rest. A flurry of shells finished our conversation, and we threw ourselves flat on the floor of the trench. Some appeared to be duds, as they whistled down and didn't explode. Later, we were told that those we thought were duds were in fact armour-piercing shells. Some went clean through the walls of the trenches, killing the men inside. I found one near our trench on my way to our shell-hole toilet.

That night I was detailed to water-party duty, collecting water from a nearby supply point behind our position. I didn't know where it was exactly but I knew it was behind enemy lines. A water pipe by the roadway was tapped during the hours of darkness, with the each of the men taking turns. It was my turn to collect the water for the runners. I moved with the runners' water bottles to join the other shadowy figures threading their way through the crawl trenches by the ADS which were filled with wounded men. It was a pitiful sight, and the stench of death and excreta was overpowering. We tried to give words of comfort and support but there was little we could do. They were in a hell of a mess. I don't know how they coped.

We moved down until we joined the others in the main party, each waiting his turn to collect water. Soon it was my turn and I moved down on to the road. The NCO held the pipe while another man took my bottles and filled them. A Bren gunner lay flat behind his gun a couple of yards away, the barrel pointing along the empty road towards the enemy. It seemed to take forever before the bottles were filled and handed back to me. This was a very tense time, four of us alone on the road under the noses of the Japs, but it was the only way to replenish our water supply. We had no choice. With the bottles filled, I quickly climbed up the hillside and rejoined the returning party. This detail would continue throughout the night, and the pipe would then be reconnected so that the supply point was kept secret from any passing Jap patrols the following day. This operation was performed nightly, and others would have to take their turn in the days to come. I was only ever ordered to go once, and it was scary, but I just filled my bottles and left. The NCO and Bren gunner were there a lot longer. I don't know if they survived but in any event they were exceptionally brave. If anyone deserved a medal at Kohima, they did.

16 APRIL

As I looked out of my trench on this day I noticed the remnants of parachutes from previous airdrops were drooped everywhere over the remaining trees. The ground was now virtually bare, all the leaf and tree cover gone. The day was quieter than usual, but of course we got the usual barrages, and the Japs carried out some probing attacks to try and find weak spots. We also received more airdrops, and these were more successful than earlier ones, most being recovered by our troops. That evening, a Supply Officer slipped us a bottle of rum as he passed and we all had a good drink. I began to feel really merry and started singing aloud, 'Onward Christian Soldiers'. Soon the others joined in until it seemed the whole hill was singing. The officers let us continue for a while, but eventually the order came to be quiet. I don't know what the Japs made of it, but we gave little thought to that. Mind you, the next barrage seemed heavier. We peered over our trench and watched the first shells and mortar bombs exploding on our forward positions, then gradually creeping up towards where we were and beyond. We counted the mortars as they came towards us. During and after each barrage you would hear the groans and moans of those that had been wounded. But we were unable to help because anyone who tried to leave his trench found himself a victim of mortar or sniper fire. It was an awful mess.

Earlier that day the Japs had positioned a machine gun among some tree cover to the rear of Keene's Bungalow (or what remained of it). It was causing a lot of problems to the Assam troops. They tried to knock it out with a mortar but that didn't work. In the end, as it got dark, four men were detailed to attack it, led by a local Naga called Angami. They left their trenches, formed up on the terrace above the Tennis Court and made a charge towards the machine gun some 40 yards down the hill. Each man held a grenade from which the release pin was removed ready to throw. A Bren gave covering fire from the left. As they ran, another Bren opened up from the Clubhouse. The Clubhouse was virtually wrecked, and the Bren gunner, Sepoy Wellington Massar, fired his weapon from the top of the billiard table to get a better field of fire, despite the fact that this was in full view of the enemy. Angami and his men completely wiped out the machine gun post but their action alerted the surrounding Jap companies, who opened fire immediately. Although Angami and his men managed to get back safely, Wellington Massar was unfortunately hit whilst covering their return. However, despite his injuries, he manned the Bren until they got back. He died later in hospital. That day, we were told that if we hung on for two more days reinforcements would arrive and we would make history.

We held on for four!

That night was dark and misty, and it rained later. The Japs repeatedly attacked the area around the Deputy Commissioner's Bungalow, now not much more than a pile of rubble, but were beaten back every time. In the early hours of the next morning, 17 April, they attacked FSD Hill, pushing A and C Companies back towards the top. A mixed group of Assam Rifles and the Assam Regiment relieved A and C and managed to retake some of the positions lost, but the Japs were still too far advanced for comfort. A and C pulled back to the southern slopes of Summerhouse Hill, a former rest area but now under constant fire. The whole area was a target and there was nowhere free from the Jap shells. My company had also suffered terrible losses, and my last run to them was to a young officer in a weapon pit with perhaps four or five men. The area had been covered with trees and vegetation at the beginning of the siege, but now the landscape was barren. There was nothing left.

When I arrived on FSD I stopped but couldn't see where anybody was. Suddenly, a corrugated sheet of metal that covered the weapon pit at ground level moved and the officer asked what I wanted. I handed over the message, which he took, his heavily bandaged wrist covering a wound of some kind. I asked if there were any snipers about and he pointed to the bullet-ridden metal dixies (cooking tins), saying that if there were, I was likely know about it fairly quickly. I didn't need any further reminder and left straight away. On the way back it dawned on me that if I hadn't been transferred from C Company Runner to BHQ Runner, I could have been, at best, in that weapon pit, where only a handful of men remained. I think the A Company runner had it worst. They stopped his runs to the Tennis Court area because of snipers, but one day towards the end of the siege he had to go down to the Tennis Court, and it was obvious he didn't fancy it. None of us would have, not amongst that lot, but he had no choice. He didn't come back. I don't know what happened to him.

Bill Cordwell was desperate for a drink and that night made his way on his own to a water point. It was a stream, no more than a trickle really. He leant over and hung his head down to quench his thirst. After a few moments he lifted his head and glanced downstream. A Jap was doing exactly the same. They looked at each other in complete surprise. I don't know if either man had any weapons with him. Bill never said what happened, but he came back. He did say once that he was close to some Jap positions and both sides had mortars but didn't use them so not to provoke retaliation.

Mind you, that didn't last long and then all hell was let loose again.

Ivan Daunt, Bernard 'Bomber' Brown, Fred Clinch and others were detailed to a water party. As previously described, the water point was away by the main road. They had to crawl to the source itself because of the fixed-line machine gun the Japs had set up. The Japs couldn't see them getting the water but fired every now and then on the off chance of catching someone. Bomber Brown collected the water bottles, but in his rush he didn't keep down and two bullets from the Jap machine gun caught him in the backside. They were only flesh wounds. The bullets didn't hit a bone, but he had to go to the ADS. Alec ('Scoffer') Longley and Dick Hook looked after him at base while the water party completed their task. Bob Clinch arranged for him to be taken to the ADS. Bob and Fred Clinch weren't the only brothers in the battalion. In fact, there were several. The Collins brothers were twins; they both got killed.

Every morning and evening the Japs sent over their barrages, as regular as clockwork. It is impossible to describe the strain we suffered. I can only liken it to being repeatedly put in front of a firing squad and then being reprieved each time. This happened twice a day, every day. The battle still raged and we watched as Allied planes swooped down through the smoke and attacked the Japs; but the enemy still kept coming, steadily pushing us back with their barrages and infantry attacks, accepting their massive losses for the small amount of ground gained. I didn't do any more runs. There was no need. The Japs had overrun our positions on the ridges all around. I spent most of the day in the trench straining my eyes to the distant roads and mountains, looking for that enemy machine gun that had pinned us down, or for a sniper. Some light relief would come as a pair of our fighters strafed the Jap positions in the hills above us with cannon and tiny flashes of fire shot up in lines across the hillside. That night, the Supply Officer gave us some cigarettes and cigars. Three Gurkhas had dug in a few yards away; they had got separated from their unit in some counter-attack, so they were now helping in defence around BHQ. Their faces showed the signs of close-quarter fighting, being pock-marked with small red cuts and scabs. We gave them the cigars. They would have preferred the cigarettes, but we kept these for ourselves.

That evening the Japs really let us have it. They attacked the area around the Tennis Court continuously, but the disciplined group of Assam Rifles and Assam Regiment fought them off. The barrage on FSD Hill went on for almost five hours, and Summerhouse Hill (where I was) copped a right pasting. We knew help was near. Some Punjabi troops were seen about half a mile to the west, working their way towards us. But we were all totally exhausted by now. We hadn't had a proper wash or sleep for over two weeks, we were bleary-eyed and wore scruffy beards. Some men were suffering from dizziness and the shakes, they were that fatigued. We didn't know if we could carry on and hold out until help arrived, but we couldn't give up. We had to dig deep, and even in these dire circumstances there were always one or two who would crack a joke or say something funny to lift morale.

Unfortunately, the Japs had more luck that night and their persistence paid off; they took FSD and advanced further to claim Kuki Piquet as well. They followed up their barrage with showers of grenades and an infantry attack with phosphorus bombs. These bombs lit up the whole area and were blinding. They set some of the remaining *bashas* alight. You could hardly see. You couldn't tell friend from foe, not until you were right next to them. Then it was too late, and hand-to-hand combat started. Tom Greatley always thought the Japs took some sort of drug, as they seemed to charge without any fear of being killed. He was convinced of this when during one charge a big Jap leading the way set off a phosphorus bomb and held it to his chest, laughing as he burnt to death. He couldn't see the reason for that. Roy Wellings also thought the Japs may have been taking something, and several times noticed that the dead had carried tiny wooden containers with a cork in the top. It may have been ceremonial. He never did find out.

Later, C Company withdrew to Summerhouse Hill. Mortar man Sergeant King had his jaw shattered by a shell splinter during the last attack on Kuki Piquet but refused to go to the ADS and remained to help his men, holding his jaw together with his hand. Blood was pouring from the wound. Eventually, he was persuaded to get treatment, only to be blown unconscious by a shell blast whilst standing by the ADS. D Company commander was also injured. The blinded Sergeant Major Haines gave a great deal of encouragement as he was led amongst the men, before the enemy eventually killed him.

We were now pushed back into an area of about 350 by 350 yards. The front line was so thin due to losses that if the Japs made a concerted effort they would surely break through, and that would be it.

Roy Wellings was alone in his trench when a Jap fell in. Fortunately, he was already dead. Roy didn't know were he came from or who'd shot him. He didn't take any chances and shot him again just to make sure. He then had to wait a few hours until it got dark before he could get him out and roll him down the slope. Needless to say, he didn't enjoy the company that day.

We could hear the sound of the 2nd British Division guns getting nearer. They had started to shell the Jap lines. We all hoped that this would weaken their positions and allow reinforcements to get through to us in time. We were told to keep well down at this time as our own artillery was now massing on the outside of Kohima and would be putting down an extremely heavy barrage on to the Japanese forward positions just a few yards in front of our own trenches. It was a heavy barrage indeed, and it was just as well that we kept right down, for as the shells landed bits of shrapnel flew all around; but we were unharmed and glad to see the Japs getting a taste of their own medicine. By now our artillery was bombarding the Japanese positions on the hillsides and their forward positions relentlessly, and our reinforcements were getting nearer every day. But the pressure on us defenders was immense, and although our losses were nothing like those of the enemy, simple arithmetic showed that it must only be a matter of time before we would be overwhelmed. For some reason they never attacked again that night, and so the line was held.

18 APRIL

This morning was cold, damp and misty. The situation was touch and go. A, C and D Companies had withdrawn to the southern slopes of Summerhouse Hill. HQ Company was around the command post area and B Company was on Hospital Ridge. We'd lost a lot of men the previous night, but our reinforcements were finally coming. The 1/1st

Punjabis were clearly visible on Piquet Hill, and eventually tanks cleared the way through with infantry support to IGH Spur. The Dimapur to Imphal Road was open again. However, the Japs were only 100 yards from the ADS and the shelling continued, each shell claiming further casualties. Ambulances arrived at the part of the road at the bottom of IGH Spur and some of the walking wounded and non-combatants walked down the road to try to leave. However, the Japs saw them and sent a barrage of shells over, wounding and killing several. The Japs also had a machine gun mounted on a nearby hillside and a number of snipers round and about. These continued to hinder the evacuation and caused further casualties. It was felt that if the Japs put in another heavy attack they would get through. I kept my magazine full with ten bullets and my bayonet fixed, in readiness for the attack that surely now must come. I also kept one bullet up the spout in case it came to hand-to-hand fighting. I'd heard that some men had got their bayonets jammed in an enemy and couldn't free them. I wasn't going to stand for that. I would free it by blasting my man off with a bullet.

There were no concerted attacks during the night of the 18th/19th until about 4.30am. Then the Japs attacked from the south, taking on an Assam Regiment unit, which was forced to withdraw through A Company's positions. The enemy took advantage of this and occupied positions only five yards in front of A Company. Then they attacked once more and managed to get in amongst A Company positions; they were now only 40 yards from BHQ. Fortunately, A Company was now supported by the 1/1st Punjabis and managed to recapture the area, killing about twenty of the enemy. A unit of Punjabis were also attacked near the Deputy Commissioner's Bungalow and suffered heavy losses, but they held firm, seeing off every Jap attack.

Superstition played a great part in some of the men's minds. Corporal Alf Judge had been put in charge of some wounded men and was detailed to help moving them with Corporal Norman, Dick Johnson and Ernie Thrussler. He was upset because he had lost his lucky teddy bear. His wife had given it to him when they parted and told him that while he had this bear he would be safe. Now he felt he was in danger without it. As he helped the wounded a Jap shell killed him. I made a mental note not to take any lucky mascots into action, should we ever get out of this mess.

All soldiers reacted differently and some seemed to show little regard for anyone. For example, a rough-and-ready Scotsman went round collecting gold teeth from dead Japs. No one said anything to him. They just let him get on with it. He would check out the body and just stamp his heel on the appropriate area to remove the tooth. I don't know what he did with them, but he had a bag full.

The local Naga tribesmen were as sometimes just as bad. They were head-hunters prior to the war and now delighted in returning back after a sortie with the ears of Japanese soldiers.

19 APRIL

This day brought more airdrops, which were very successful considering the restricted area left for the planes to aim at, though there were inevitably casualties caused by the falling supplies, due to the concentration of men. Still no reinforcements had arrived, but we fought on. There was no other way. We knew that if the 2nd Division didn't take control that day it would be all over for us. Meanwhile, they sent barrage after barrage into the Jap positions. The guns were positioned behind each other on the main road outside our perimeter because the sides of the road were flanked by steep slopes. Shells were meticulously guided to their targets by the ever-present Yeo; 25lb shells ripped into the enemy positions and our Hurribombers relentlessly deposited their bombs. Barrett's Indians and non-combatants continued their magnificent job of ferrying the wounded down to the waiting ambulances and trucks, under the constant threat of mortar and sniper fire. Many of the wounded were killed or wounded again, and the majority of the loading party themselves became casualties. Those killed couldn't be buried due to the Jap snipers, and the Indians were ordered to just collect them for burial later.

That night we prepared for the worst, but the Japs attacks didn't have their usual ferocity. We were grateful for that because our defences were so thin that any attack of substance would have succeeded. The command bunker itself was severely damaged by the constant shelling, and Ivan Daunt and the other Pioneers had a hell of a job keeping it repaired. But there were no more infantry attacks.

Snipers were still active, though, and unfortunately Major Harry Smith and Tom Coath were wounded. Harry was talking to Colonel Richards at the entrance to his dugout, when he got hit just above the cheek; a fragment of shrapnel was stuck there. He was given a shot of morphia at the casualty point and the next thing he recalled was seeing the clean uniforms of the 2nd Division's Royal Berkshires making their way up the hill the next morning. Bill Wykes was in a forward bunker by the Deputy Commissioner's Bungalow with head cover and a slit in the front for fire and observation. He peered over the top to see what was going on, heard a swish, and then a bullet smacked into the rear of the bunker. A Jap sniper must have seen his face but his aim wasn't that good. Bill didn't let that happen again. Brummie-born Harry Hopkins wasn't so lucky; he was killed.

20 APRIL

The men of the 1st Battalion of the Royal Berkshire Regiment relieved us on 20 April 1944. They couldn't believe what they saw. Many of them were retching as they approached our positions. The rancid smell of dead bodies and excreta greeted them, together with the awful sights of death and carnage. We gave them what advice we could. We had to, as we couldn't let them face the Japs without telling them what to expect. At least the Royal Berks were better equipped. They had new, more modern weapons, rather than the old Lee Enfield rifles with long bayonets that we were using. Some had flamethrowers.

The RWKs started moving out down IGH Spur. I went with Ron Clayton and the other surviving runners to join the remainder of the BHQ and HQ and the rest of the Battalion rifle companies, plus the walking wounded. Ivan Daunt got out of his weapon pit, leaving his mates Horace Collins and one of the Browns behind. Horace was dead but they hadn't had chance to bury him. Bernard Brown was wounded. Horace and Bernard had been packing up, getting ready to move out. Horace was out of his trench when a Jap sniper got him. Bernard Brown heard Horace cry out and looked over the parapet of the trench to see what was happening. The same sniper caught him in the left shoulder. His mates dressed his wound and took him to the

ADS. (Horace's brother Len had been killed a few days earlier but he didn't know about it. We were going to tell him when we'd got out). The Japs continued to shell and snipe at us as we left, causing further casualties. Even the wounded weren't spared, and some were killed or wounded again as they were put on to the waiting lorries. Corporal Les Rose was killed before we left. Private Walter Forsyth died a couple of days after being taken out.

As we moved down the hill to the lorries, I noticed that the whole area was virtually barren; the trees and vegetation had been blasted away, and just jagged spikes remained of the previous tree cover. Parachutes from previous airdrops hung on some of those trees, their contents long gone. We continued down IGH Spur to a sheltered gully with cliff-like sides, finding dead Japs here and there. The upper parts of a dead Jap were propped up against the bank in part of the gully; just the chest, shoulders and head – his lower torso and legs were completely missing. The debris of war was everywhere: Jap bodies, helmets, rubbish, everything. We were the lucky ones.

Sherman tanks pointed their guns at the Jap positions to protect the withdrawal and the 2nd Division troops moving up to take over our positions. The trucks were waiting on the road at the end of the gulley. Their clean-shaven drivers and others looked on in amazement as they helped us aboard. We didn't think of ourselves as heroes, but these men did. They clapped and cheered us as we came down. 'Shabash, Royal West Kents!' the Indians shouted. Everyone looked at us in surprise, not expecting heroes to look so unshaven, dirty and long-haired, stinking from being unable to wash and red-eyed from lack of sleep. We were lost in our own thoughts and took no notice. We just settled down in the trucks, then fell asleep with fatigue straight away as they trundled down the mountain road towards Dimapur.

A few miles later we were woken up for a meal and some tea, then set off again back to a base near Dimapur for a longer rest. We then slept through the next 24 hours, missing meals despite being called and woken up for them. Several razor blades were needed to shave off the beards grown during the Siege, and we cleaned ourselves up. It was strange; we weren't used to it.

Two lorries turned up with big copper tanks. They parked and set up showers between them. They were hot too, though I don't know where they got the hot water. I didn't care. Actually they were too hot, but it didn't matter, we felt a lot better for it.

Some of the men had to shave their bodies because of lice and other insects. We were all sprayed with some type of DDT or disinfectant.

After 24 hours we were called into a large marquee. The CO, Laverty, told us what we had achieved in buying time for others to arrive and halt the Japanese advance on India. He told us he had been awarded the DSO, but said it was for all of us, not just him.

The sixteen-day Siege had cost the RWKs dearly: 80 of our men had been killed and nearly 200 wounded. Corporal Norman and others went to visit some of the wounded in a Dimapur hospital. They were shocked to find wounded men still in a state, unwashed and with their old dirty dressings. They complained to our officers and the matter was taken to GHQ. The wounded were looked after properly after that.

Chapter 7

Recuperation and Advance

We were still in a rest area when a new NCO detailed me and some others to watch out for enemy aircraft in case of an air raid. He gave me a whistle to blow should I spot any, but we were allowed to wander around while on duty, doing our own thing, and we hadn't seen any enemy planes for weeks. Then one day I spotted a group of aircraft in steady formation over Kohima. Suddenly there were loud explosions as bombs were dropped. I blew my whistle and raced to my trench.

The NCO appeared at my side saying, 'Bit late with that whistle weren't you, Street?'

'I thought they were ours', I replied, as we dived into our trench.

Jap fighters then started to strafe the nearby road below us, and as one flew over our heads I slammed a couple of shots into it quickly, aiming at its wings, but it was gone in seconds. Another circled round, climbing higher to clear the trees. I sent more shots into its fuselage, but the plane soon disappeared from view. All was then quiet, as tank guns and rifle fire stopped; but a minute or two later, I spotted what I thought was another Jap plane flying on the course set by those we had just fired at. It seemed slower, as if searching for a target, coming in from behind a group of trees. I quickly decided to take a really good aim at this one, put my hand up to take the range and fired straight at the cockpit. To my horror I then saw the RAF markings on the fighter, which started to waggle his wings to signal that he was friendly. But it was too late; all the other rifles in the valley had opened up. However, the tanks didn't fire, nor did our automatic weapons, as they recognized him immediately. Fortunately, he flew off to safety. We didn't see any more planes after that.

After Kohima we had a new NCO, a hard but fair man. His method of 'on parade, on parade' and 'off parade, off parade' worked well with the men. He was a loyal man to his troops and once, when drinking in a bar with some of them on leave, knocked a chap out for criticizing his West Kents.

It was May 1944 when we moved back towards Kohima, and the monsoon rain had started again. The Japs were retreating and many were trapped trying to break out back to their own lines. Others had fled into the hills. Although in a rest area, we were just behind the front line and could hear much of the action in the distance. At one point our chaps hit a Jap ammunition dump and we were treated to a spectacular 'firework' display, with explosions and fires burning continuously for three days and nights.

We took a route north of Kohima, heading towards the Jessami Track, which started by the Kohima cemetery, with its English-style gravestones, and ran through thickly wooded and jungle-ridden mountainsides. We passed a burnt-out British tank with a shell hole in the back of its turret. Later, we moved over an old Jap position and found there the bodies of about thirty British and Indians on the slopes, now just uniforms and bones.

On the top of a ridge was a row of blown-out Jap bunkers, their contents looking like something out of a horror film. Dead Japs' skulls grinned from under their helmets as their bodies sprawled around in the bottom of their positions. We went on by, happy that our chaps on the slopes hadn't died in vain. We later passed through some of the 2nd Division's Worcestershire Regiment positions and I saw some old friends from my Norton Barracks days, including Private Hill. I stopped for a rest and a natter with him about old times, during which he dropped mortar bombs down the barrel of his weapon and fired them at the enemy. Without breaking sentence, he would simply adjust the sight and continue firing as we talked.

We stayed the night where we were and then at first light moved down to join the Jessami Track. We walked in single file. I was at the head of the column with the other members of Signals Platoon and the CO. Mules were the main (sometimes the only) form of transport, carrying food, provisions and equipment on the mountain tracks. The tracks we used were wide enough to let other mules pass, but with only very little room to spare. We all felt sorry for the mules with their heavy loads but we had a love-hate relationship with them and their muleteers. Sometimes the animals' loud braying would give away our position, but we needed them. The muleteers themselves would fuss over their charges and scratch around for extra food or titbits to feed them, almost treating them as pets. They were really devoted to them, so much so that I remember seeing a muleteer crying, poor chap, because one of his mules had fallen over the edge of track and down the mountainside, dragging two others with it.

After a few days we joined up with one of the SAS-type units. They were fresh-faced young lads who hadn't been in the jungle long, but they had cleared that part of the Jessami Track of Japs. One early misty morning at first light we arrived at an abandoned Japanese camp. The enemy had departed in a hurry, leaving everything as it was. They couldn't have been gone long. A billycan of water was still boiling on the fire, rifles were stacked neatly in threes and uniforms were still hanging on bushes. I kicked the tin into the fire and we took the bolts out of the rifles and threw them down the jungle-covered hillside. We went through the pockets of the uniforms for information, but most were empty.

A dead Jap lay on a stretcher and I walked past, leaving him alone but kicking a bloodstained white rag on the ground as I went by. My friend behind picked it up and to my disappointment shook it out to find it was a large Japanese battle flag with a tiger on it, a fine souvenir, nice and light and easy to carry. We continued to search the camp, but found nothing and started to go back, only to find the 'dead' Jap had got up and gone. He had been lying doggo, waiting for an opportunity to escape. We wouldn't be so casual next time!

Japanese units were holding the mountainside positions at the edge of the main Imphal Road going back towards Kohima, and as we moved lower down we got a view of the heavy guns firing up at these roadside enemy positions. A few hours later, we heard Vickers heavy machine guns firing. (It was 6 June 1944, D-Day. We heard that the Allies had invaded Europe, and although happy to hear the news, wished we could get more help out here, feeling that we were not getting the praise or back-up we deserved). Helped by airdrops of food and ammunition, we joined others and then moved on further down the Imphal Road and within hours arrived at Imphal. This capital of the semi-independent Indian state of Manipur was a small town with a large British base, an airstrip and a tented hospital. It was situated on the Imphal plain, an oval, somewhat bowl-shaped plateau surrounded by mountain ranges covered in woodland, thigh-high grass and jungle. In the monsoon season the plains would flood and look like a huge lake enclosed by the mountains.

We headed for a rest area before pushing forward west of Imphal to clear a route called the Silchar Track (Silchar being another Jap-occupied area). This track left Imphal and headed west into the mountains, curving back towards the Dimapur–Imphal Road and the plain of Imphal, a flat country of paddy fields, with the roadway itself built up high above them so it could be used when they were flooded. Nagas and other tribal people, mostly women, were at the roadside selling fruit and vegetables in big plaited bamboo baskets. They were dressed in their traditional red-patterned, almost Red Indian-style blankets, which were draped over their shoulders, with black plaited pigtails hanging down on either side of their bronze faces. This 'Wild West' appearance was completed by a feather in the hair and trailing earrings. The men carried a shotgun or a spear, and most had a tinderbox and flint; they would often light our cigarettes for us after the rain had soaked through our clothes, ruining our matches.

We reached the rest site, where we stayed for a day or so and were issued with monsoon capes, before we moved up into some high mountains around the Silchar Track. The monsoon season was producing sudden downpours of rain and spells of sunshine in the day. It seemed like there was more rain after dark, but I suppose it was just the same really, wet and dry spells throughout the twenty-four hours. As the monsoon continued, the lashing rains caused landslides. Lorries slid all over the place and those towing guns were almost impossible to control. Often we would help to keep guns connected to their vehicles and on the road by holding on to ropes, whilst the drivers wrestled with the steering wheel.

In the early hours we moved over the open grassy mountainsides with a lot of dead ground dropping away out of sight. It was a land of streams and ravines, with very few trees and slippery, greasy long grass, about eighteen inches high. These were days of never getting dry and having permanently wet feet. We would sleep in wet clothes and blankets, with water running underneath us as we dozed. Small leeches would wave backwards and forwards on the tips of the grass and many found a place inside our boots by slipping through the lace holes. They would suck our blood, but we didn't feel them as they were crushed in our socks; we would only discover the telltale bloodstains in our shoes and socks when they were removed.

Fear of our unknown future meant we took little heed of our present discomfort. We almost accepted it all as a part of the life we were leading; eating, sleeping and, most of all, trying to stay alive. We longed to hear those magic words, 'Leave in India'. We would sit on guard each night, on the edge of a trench half filled with water, drenched by the monsoon rains, and just let our minds drift. It would be two in the morning and my thoughts would go back to Birmingham. Our time zone was five hours ahead and I would think of what was happening at home: Dad would be getting his last pint of beer to take home from the outdoor before it shut; Mom would be preparing supper.

On one occasion I was singing a song to myself, when I suddenly heard a noise. My whole body tensed up and I readied myself, slipping off the safety catch of my rifle, dropping to my knees in our water-filled trench and staring into the darkness. I thanked God it was warm, as standing in that water for up to two hours at a time whilst on guard duty would otherwise have been unbearable. I relaxed as all remained quiet. I then waited to be relieved so I could get some sleep. But sleep would only be for two hours as my next stint was at four in the morning, at which time we would have to stand to in case of a dawn attack. Then it would be a quick breakfast of soya sausage links and beans, help load the mules and off again, marching on to rejoin the Imphal Road.

I was twenty-four years old now, but felt a hundred. All of us young men had seen too much in too short a time. I believe they called it living a lifetime in a day. I don't know about that, but what we had seen during the last few months was enough for anyone. Home seemed far away, just a dream. Fatigue would often take over, causing confusion. Was this a dream or was this home? You didn't really know, but you couldn't let these thoughts overcome you and so you took a grip, forcing them out of your mind. You brought in new ones, like a meal at Firpo's when the leave that we longed for so much eventually came through. Then suddenly another noise would be heard and the tension returned; you became a soldier again, no time for thinking.

Our officers in the lead must either have had a guide or worked from a map and compass as we climbed up the mountainside. The greasy mud covered the wet grass, making the climb harder for us soldiers weighed down with extra rations, ammunition, grenades and our rifles. Bill Cordwell, who was with us, was in MT (Motor Transport) Section. He had driven lorries in France and the Middle East, but it was mules here. The mules carried boxes of ammunition, tents, bedding, cooking equipment and all the other things needed to keep a busy army unit in action. In spite of their heavy loads they were sure-footed on the grassy slopes, and some soldiers hung on to their tails to heave themselves up the steepest parts. Many of us couldn't bring ourselves to do this; the poor mules had enough weight to carry without us adding to their troubles. I don't know what we would have done without them. They brought us the supplies that were dropped further back by American and British planes.

We rested where we stood and just lay down to sleep in our monsoon capes in the pouring rain. The mules weren't unloaded and just stood there. We only had a couple of hours' sleep or rest – no meals or tea, nothing else. I felt sorry for all of us, more so the mules, but we grabbed what rest we could and soon were on our way again. The column of men and mules left in a long single file along the narrow, muddy, rain-lashed, leech-infested track. We were so tired, past caring about being hungry and wet as the rainwater poured down our steel helmets and monsoon capes on to our uniforms . We were wet through, but when daylight came the hot sunshine dried us out and, more importantly, dried our blankets.

When we arrived near the peak of the mountains, we followed the Silchar Track for a few miles, then spread out in defensive positions. We crossed a deep *chaung*, more of a ravine really, with hardly any water in it because there was little rain now. The early monsoon seemed to have stopped, except for the odd shower.

We took up our position on a large peak. There were only a few trees around and these were not as high as some we had passed earlier. The Japs had dug bunkers under them. We reached our proposed BHQ and Company HQ positions and settled in by the track. Others spread out overlooking the ravine. Thankfully, C Company were to the rear, a few hundred yards behind BHQ and Company HQ. Other Companies were at the front and in flanking positions on the dead ground which sloped away.

The rain, when it came, didn't seem so heavy, so I didn't wear my monsoon cape on runs to my Company. Most of my runs were now straightforward. I crossed to a nearby ravine and followed a well-worn track sloping downwards at the bottom of it. Then it was through the wild bushes and small tree growth either side of a little track and on down this long, gentle slope to a dry riverbed full of bushes and trees. I followed the windings of the streambed, and it widened as I climbed out the other side, being 30 feet deep at that point. This was a dangerous place that could hide many Japs. The idea of being caught at the bottom, should any Japs appear, was frightening. I did my runs and didn't hang around, carrying my messages as fast and as carefully as I could.

All went well for a few days, until one day when I heard noises in the *chaung* and slowed down. I crept quietly forward, lowering myself to a prone position near the edge of the ravine, my rifle at the ready. To my relief I saw three wild pigs, a large boar and a sow with a little piglet, all snorting and rooting around in the bushes at the bottom of the ravine. I took aim at the boar but decided against firing, thinking, 'OK, I could shoot the pig, but if I miss, the bullet will whine around, someone might get edgy on the hill and it could draw fire from anyone, comrade or enemy alike.' Anyway, odd Jap groups or patrols could have been drawn to any rifle fire. The pigs made my mind up for me; getting my scent, they raced off at speed into the bushes, squealing and grunting. I moved down the ravine, got out again and returned to BHQ. When I got back I told them about the pigs, and they were not pleased. They felt that a nice bit of pork would have made a welcome change from our normal rations.

On another occasion, before we advanced further, I was sent to bring the officers of the other RWK Companies to BHQ for briefing and to study 'mud maps'. These were fascinating models in mud of the surrounding terrain, from which the CO would explain to the officers how and when we would move forward.

Another time, coming back from a run to my Company I heard the sound of a cart or a gun being moved, a rattle of wheel noise in the dead ground near an old Jap position. The terrain hid whatever it was from my sight, but I moved up towards the side of a peak with old Jap bunkers on top to get a better look; from there I thought I could spot or even fire at this hidden vehicle. As the noise from the dead ground got nearer and nearer I suddenly realized that I wouldn't reach the bunkers in time – they were too high up. It was clear to me that I would be visible on the open high ground, so I stopped where I was for a few minutes. I nervously waited and let whoever it was continue on their way, both of us hidden from the other's view, then calmly moved down the track back to my Company HQ on the hill.

The next day, after taking a message to my Company I had good news: my leave had come through and they gave me a list of places in India that I could visit. This was my first leave after over six months in action, and I set off with several other men from my unit to the hill station at Simla. I didn't return to the Silchar Track area. After my leave I would rejoin my unit on their advance south of Imphal down the Tiddim Road. While 60 or 70 miles of that road remained in the state of Manipur, the remaining 40 miles were over the border in Burma, and it crossed the Manipur River en route.

Chapter 8

Leave in Simla

Simla was over 2,000 miles from where we were on the Silchar Track west of Imphal, and to get there we had travel overland. First we headed for the border between the princely state of Manipur and the rest of British India, starting with a six-hour hike down the mountainsides, in the monsoon. To add to our difficulties we were handed a Bren gun to take back for repair, to be left at the Admin Company, somewhere on the Imphal plains near the road. A guide led us slipping, sliding and falling down the mountainsides and crossing fast flowing mountain streams of white water, in which it was hard to keep our balance. Although these streams were narrow, we could only cross them slowly because of the strong current.

High in the mountains, we looked down on the Imphal plain, with its clusters of villages and palm trees dotted all over the place. The paddy fields were now flooded and the plain looked like one big lake, with mountains rising all around, stretching into the far distance and out of sight. We were covered in mud by the time we got down to meet the waiting lorry which would take us to Admin Company. We saw the Quartermaster there, changed our uniforms and socks and got money for our leave, together with passes for the trains. We stayed overnight there, then took another lorry to Dimapur railway station after breakfast the next morning.

Our group were put under a tall, easy-going Scottish NCO, who had seen action in the Arakan with the tall soldiers of the West African Division. While we waited for our train, we chatted to him and exchanged stories.

The station was packed full of soldiers in jungle green. We stood around in groups chatting, our bedding roles and packs on the ground beside us. Then a strange soldier appeared. He was thickset and wearing a KD (khaki drill) off-white uniform, a pre-war style that you saw in some of the Indian garrison towns far from the front line. He stood out like a sore thumb in our crowd of jungle-green uniforms. Sporting a silver-knobbed cane, he marched up to us and started telling us how smart his old regiment was. He told us that you had to be smart and march properly on parade, then showed us how by marching up and down the platform. Our Scottish NCO grinned and winked at us as the Redcaps (military police) marched this strange character away. It was never explained to me what he was up to.

Our tins of rations arrived and we loaded them on to the train together with tea, sugar and tins of milk for making tea along the way. We then found our seats. We didn't know it then, but this journey would end at the Brahmaputra River several hours away. Getting off the train, we boarded an old paddle steamer that looked like something out of a Mississippi Western, a picture we fitted quite well with our bush hats and bedding rolls slung over our shoulders. The officers looked even more the part, with their pistols on their hips, some tied down in holsters on their thighs like the old-fashioned gunslingers. To me the whole scene was like a picture out of the comic magazines I used to read as a kid. It was almost unreal.

We found a space on the deck and laid out our ground sheets and blankets to rest, using our packs as pillows. Being on leave, we had no rifles, and our small packs contained mess tins, knife, fork and spoon and a tin mug for tea. A cooked meal was prepared for us at least once a day on the boat, but we still had plenty of tinned food in our rations and hot tea for in-between times. We had plenty of cigarettes to smoke, and these were lazy days to catch up on some welcome sleep. There were no guards, and we relaxed as the boat made its way down the river, which was very wide, perhaps a mile or so across, and flooded with the monsoon rains. Now and then the paddle steamer blasted off its horn to warn other boats. The echo of that sound gave the feeling of vast space around us. The river was very big, as were its fish. Now and then we would look over the side and see very large black fish of some kind, which sank below the surface some yards in front of us when they heard the steamer coming.

We took it easy whilst we could, and forty-eight hours later we reached our destination, another railhead, then boarded the train to Calcutta. Somehow I caught a cold on this train; it seemed as if our lazy style of life had allowed dormant germs to come to the surface, but I soon recovered. We still took our daily mepacrine tablets to keep malaria at bay, our skins now turning yellow from their continual use.

When we arrived in Calcutta, we settled into an Army rest camp of *bashas* containing typical Indian wooden string beds with coconut fibre mattresses. An organized cookhouse gave us meals three times a day. The camp had an M.O. and all the mod cons, even pay parades. After booking in we left to visit Chowringee. We had waited a long time for this. Chowringee was a main road of hotels, barbers, picture houses and other places of amusement. Most of us went to Firpo's Hotel as it was said to be the place to go. A door with the name 'Firpo's' above it led us up a wide staircase and into a large, long room with rows of tables in typical English style, each set with a snowy white linen tablecloth. It was a right posh affair. We were ushered to tables, each with a waiter and bearer wearing a white turban, a clean white tunic-style coat and a red sash. They handed us the menus and we settled down to a meal of duck with green peas and potatoes, washed down with a few bottles of ice-cold beer. We spoilt ourselves rotten.

Afterwards, we went to an air-conditioned picture house. As we sat in comfort I noticed a shelf was provided in front of the seats for the cold drinks which were sent to us as we sat watching the film. We even went to an old fashioned barber's shop for a haircut and shave, with hot face towels. We couldn't believe it. It was like something out of the old cowboy films. But I had waited a long time for this and remembered my thoughts as we were trapped in our trenches at Kohima. I was determined to enjoy it. I now realized how uncertain the future was and seized the moment. The Japs couldn't take this away.

However, outside these luxurious establishments beggars would sit around in the street, and we gave them a few *annas* of change before continuing on our way to join a mass of other soldiers sightseeing and watching the rickshaw-*wallahs* ply for trade alongside street traders with all sorts of things to sell. It seemed that the men of a dozen nations were here: Yanks, British, Indians of all sorts, both Air Force and Army. Some men took a chance to break bounds and visit prostitutes. Many got away with it, not catching anything, but most stayed in the designated areas.

It was here that I realized the world was a small place. I met a chap who lived round the corner from us in Birmingham. He was in some other mob somewhere else along the Burma front line. It amazed me that I could meet a person half way across the world who lived so close to me at home. I'd never seen him before and I never saw him again.

From Howra railway station, where for a few coins the local children helped carry our packs and bedding rolls, we left to go on to New Delhi. We boarded the carriages distinctly marked in white letters 'BOR' (British Other Ranks) and after two days arrived at another rest camp before taking our next train. We had to wait a further three days before it came. Two days and two trains later, we arrived in New Delhi.

We asked the RTO Officer when the next train left for Simla and found we would have a day to look round New Delhi before catching an overnight train. New Delhi was more organized than towns and cities we had experienced elsewhere, a far cry from the hurly-burly of Calcutta. After our day around the town, we boarded the mountain train to Simla.

Once aboard, our bearer said that breakfast would be served at four in the morning. We were woken up with a slice of toast, a pot of tea, sugar, milk and hot water, all on a neat tray. Quite a change from having breakfast sitting on the ground in the jungle or at the bottom of a trench, rushing to eat it before someone wanted a hand to load a mule or the order came to stand to.

When we reached Simla we left the train and met the lady in whose bungalow we were staying. We handed over 30 rupees each for our stay for the following two weeks. Whilst relaxing we discussed, and daydreamed of the chances of the monsoon rains giving rise to landslides, causing road and rail services to be disrupted so that we could stay extra weeks while repairs took place. Wishful thinking!

In Simla we got the same warning about staying in pairs as we had had at other hill stations; about the high roads and overhanging cliffs where there was the possibility of attack by panthers and other wild animals. All around were pine forests, and these stretched towards the wild land around the distant snow-clad mountains, miles away in the background. We looked over a small wall and down a steep slope at the treetops of the pine forest. The big light-grey monkeys were as surprised as we were to see each other and would leap and bound through the treetops chattering continuously.

The next morning, the bungalow lady said we could have as much buttered toast and tea as we liked and we should just to call the bearer or servant to get it for us. We had already sampled a bowl of the native porridge with milk and sugar. It was horrible, but we found a small shop between the bungalow and the town that served English food: bacon, eggs, bread, tea and coffee. So each day, after a piece of toast and a cup of tea, we went there for a full English breakfast. Then we would walk around the town and make our way to the bazaar to do some souvenir shopping. At the bazaar you could buy gifts or clothes to send home, and there was even a place to get photos taken of ourselves. I had one taken and sent it home to my mother. I also bought a new bush jacket, trousers and side hat in creamy brown khaki drill. The bush jacket had long sleeves to roll up during the day or to bring down at night to protect my arms from mosquitoes. All this cost only thirty rupees and, with free alterations, was fitted and ready to collect in two hours.

Simla was a hill station where the Europeans in India sent their families in the very hot months of the Indian summer, before the monsoon broke. Its English-style churches, bungalows and restaurants, the cooler evenings, the English summer conditions and the clear, clean air blowing from the snow-covered mountains made it a place for a welcome relaxation. A typical evening out would be a visit to the picture house, followed by a meal. During our stay we were invited to the Vice-regal Lodge, with its silver thrones used by the Viceroy and his lady. They weren't there themselves, and others were in charge when we arrived. They passed us over to guides, native servants and bearers. These were thickset Sikhs of military bearing, dressed up in their regal red tunic-style uniforms with gold coats of arms embroidered on the chests, beautiful gold sashes and gold and red turbans.

We were shown around the throne room and admired the large padded armchair-style silver thrones. Our uniformed servant/guide trusted us to look around on our own, and when he left us alone for a while many of us took the opportunity to try out the silver thrones for size. Soon we became bored with the throne room, and our guide took us to a large lounge, where we had tea and a chat with relatives and friends of the Viceroy. They introduced us to a troupe of English and Anglo-Indian cancan dancers who were to perform for us. We felt like Royalty, being treated so well by these upper-class people.

Unfortunately, our leave passed all too quickly and soon we were back on the train to the front line. On the way we stopped at yet another rest camp. It was hot and dusty, unlike the McPherson Barracks at Allahabad with its modern football and hockey pitches and tennis courts. There we had had the luxury of being shaved in bed in the early morning and our kit cleaned, with a fresh change of uniform twice a day, morning and evening, all delivered by the laundryman (or *dhobi*, as he was called). The clothes were neatly placed at the end of our beds, and our boots were polished and ready to wear. There was even a barber and a tailor there, and we had handmade shoes for evening wear. We led the life of gentlemen and would relax on the veranda outside, attended by our *char-wallah* (tea and cakes) and a fruit-*wallah*. This place was distinctly different and nowhere near as comfortable. Simple *bashas* provided our accommodation, with roughly covered separate toilets and shower blocks.

Soon after we got there we met our old friend, the NCO who had originally come out from England to India with us. He had been wounded at Kohima and his wound had got him a downgrade from the infantry and a safe job on the rest camp. He was still one of the lads and looked after us, arranging a pay parade as we hadn't been paid for weeks. He told us that there was another train later that week, so we didn't have to rush and could have an extra day or two at the rest camp, away from the front line, knowing what we had been through. We followed the same route back by train to Calcutta, then train again, followed by the paddle steamer. It all seemed to have gone so fast. We disembarked to get the train back to Dimapur. We had a further night in a rest camp there and then continued back through Kohima and Imphal and on to BHQ.

Chapter 9

The Chocolate Staircase

The Silchar track had been cleared of Japs by the time we returned to continue our advance down the Tiddim Road south of Imphal. I was still retained as C Company's Runner and after returning from leave was apprehensive about it, but there was no easy way back into the job. The monsoon was still in full swing when I started by doing a run the very next day. The mud was so deep it covered my boots. I had to get from our BHQ roadside defensive positions to the forward position of my Company, along a trail deep in the mountains. The roads were thick with liquid mud and the lorries struggled. There was no room for error as there was a sheer drop at the road edge.

We had a rest while another battalion took the lead for a few days, and we received some canteen goods, extra canned fruit and a bottle of beer. The cooks prepared some dehydrated potatoes, onions and mutton for the last hot meal of the day. We washed that down with a mug of hot tea. Then we took our mepacrine tablets to ward off malaria and used our mugs for the rum ration. Darkness fell. The guards were set for the night. No sudden attacks were expected but we still stood to in our trenches. Although many Japanese were dying from starvation and disease, thousands were still falling back in retreat and were scattered all over the place, so we couldn't take any chances.

Some of us were allowed to stand down, but others remained at their posts. We took our turn later, in trenches which held six inches of water in the bottom. We had pitched our two-man tents on a level piece of ground scraped out near the slit trench we'd dug. These tents had been carried on mules during the day as we advanced, and they provided us with shelter when resting in between stints of guard duty at night. As dawn broke we would wash and shave; there was now no shortage of water compared with Kohima (the monsoon made sure of that). We then got ready to move on. We had travelled almost 100 miles over parts of a road where battles old and new had left bodies in varying states of decay, some fresh, others just bones. At that time I shared my two-man tent with a Scot from Edinburgh, a quiet man with a middle class accent. I liked him and we got on fine. I would moan about this and that and he would agree. We didn't fall out or upset each other. That was important.

We had to get to the Manipur River, but in front of us was a twenty-mile 'bush' typhus belt, a real concern to the African soldiers. The British troops seemed to recover better from this illness, whereas many of the Africans died. They were superstitious about these tropical diseases and would give up the fight to live. It was said to be caught from a rat or from a bug or flea that lived on the tips of the long grass; these attacked bare arms unprotected by sleeves, which were rolled up in the hot climate of the jungle. We were given oil to rub into our arms every day to protect us and were ordered to keep the long sleeves of our jungle-green tunics rolled down, but some still caught it. At dusk, swarms of small flies would suddenly rise in clouds. They got everywhere. They bit your backside if you went to the toilet, so I made sure I didn't go at that time. They even got under your helmet and didn't half make your head itch. They only came out in the early evening and disappeared as quickly as they came. We were glad when we left them behind.

We halted for a night near the banks of the Manipur River, dug in and pitched our tents. We were to cross it the next day. There was no bridge and we heard the roar of the fast flowing river long before we saw it. The floodwater was sand-coloured, white in places, and showed its strength by juggling the tree trunks floating down it. A boat appeared from somewhere, and some Indian soldiers used to flooded rivers managed to swim over with a cable to help bring it across. I don't know how they managed it. The current was horrendous. The rope or cable they took with them was wrapped round a thick tree trunk on the far bank, and a group of our soldiers boarded the boat and started to pull it across. Part of the way over, the boat tipped up and the men fell into the river. It was chaos as the vicious current washed these poor chaps away. Quite a few were missing, and patrols were sent to search the banks. Some were found with broken arms where large rocks dragged down by the flooded waters had smashed into them. Those were the lucky ones; others drowned. My little friend from Scotland was in that boat and went missing, presumed drowned. His body was never found. The water had risen over side of the boat as they pulled it across, flooding it and causing it to capsize.

I was detailed to cross on a second boat and hoped that the people in charge had learnt their lesson. We took no chances, removing our gaiters so that if the water got into our trousers it wouldn't be caught in them. We carried all our packs and pouches, but they were loose and ready to throw off in case we had to swim for the bank should the boat capsize. I had an awful feeling of being expendable, but didn't show it. We got into the boat, and as we waited I said a little prayer. We moved slowly across the river and as we got nearer the middle the water started to climb higher and higher up the boat's sides. We were all worried. It was only inches from the gunwale, but to our relief it slowly dropped again. We got across unharmed. The rest of the group crossed safely over the next few hours.

On the other side I discovered a group of dead Japs in an open space about 30 or 40 feet from the river bank. They were long dead, just bones. I picked up a small ivory rod around three inches long which looked like a thick pen. It was a Japanese family name stamp and I kept it for a souvenir. When everybody was finally across we moved away from the river, which soon began to look like a silver thread of cotton behind us, weaving its way through the mountains. In front of us the road followed a large horseshoe shape and we moved into a position covered with jungle and long grass along the mountainside overlooking the road. We now went forward into Japanese-held territory. It was four in the afternoon and I was sent on a run with a message to my Company, having to return in the dark through unknown enemy-held territory. I didn't like that.

We were told that some women bearers were to help us carry our equipment. We were excited at this prospect, but when they turned up we discovered they were 'old hags' in their fifties, led by an old man. They were good bearers, though.

There were breaks in our advance down the road; whilst dug in on a mountainside overlooking the road another infantry unit passed through the mountains and around us to take the lead. We were told that we would be resting where we were for a few days. That suited us. We received some mail and made sure we got some rest and sleep. We also took the opportunity to write letters. Some got parcels from home and local papers. We also got more to eat and a bottle of beer from the airdrop area. These were brought up by mules and lorries which worked relentlessly in the pouring monsoon rains.

In the evening we had our rum ration and went through the routine of taking our malaria tablets and rubbing ointment into our arms to protect us from typhus. In the daytime we took life easy when we could. On one occasion I walked round and looked at a group of mules tethered to a clump of trees, feeding. They seemed to see me or at least sense me watching. I was perhaps too close to them, and they moved almost as one, bringing their rear ends slowly round to my direction, as if to warn me. I kept my distance, as the last thing I needed was for one of them to lash out with its hooves and injure me. I realized that they needed time and space as well, so I left them in peace.

That evening, Japs started shelling the land near our rest area, reminding us they were still out there and knew where we were. We moved out the next day. We pushed on towards Tiddim, some 40 miles south of the Manipur River. The next target would be the Third Stockade, further down the road south of Tiddim. This was a Japanese supply base, where they kept food stores consisting of sacks of rice, a form of cocoa powder and tins of mixed meat and cherries, amongst other things. We had to capture this place to break the supply lines to the Japanese defences. Seven miles south of Tiddim was at the start of the 'Chocolate Staircase', where the road was built up the side of a mountain in a series of hairpin bends, seemingly taking the form of an enormous staircase. This and the sickly, reddish-brown mud gave the place its nickname. A mile beyond the top of the 'Staircase'was a well defended high mountain top called Kennedy Peak. From here the Japanese could view the road for miles. That had to be captured too.

We moved out in sections, passing the bloated dead bodies of

Japanese stragglers on either side of the road. Sick or wounded, they had died where they fell. The smell of death was with us all the time as we passed the rotting bodies of friend or foe, you couldn't tell really which, often just some bones in a uniform, unrecognizable by now.

As we pushed on I met a soldier called Preston who lived around the corner at home in Birmingham and was married with a small child. He joined us, and when we stopped to strike camp we talked about home. I remember that he always sang a particular song, one that he had sung to his wife – 'Bless You for Being an Angel'. It was his favourite, and he often sang it whilst putting up the tent or during the singsongs we used to have. He was killed later, shot in error by one of our own chaps with a Sten gun. It was a terrible business, but these guns were always a problem, often jamming or firing at the slightest jolt. Many a dispatch rider would be riding his motorcycle over a bump in the road and hear the sound of automatic machine gun fire, only to realize it was his own weapon. Poor Preston had been standing in front of a bloke cleaning his gun, when it went off for no apparent reason. He caught a short burst of bullets to the stomach.

I was still C Company Runner and my work was never done. It seemed harder to leave this rest area in mid-afternoon, but that was when I got orders to take a message to my forward Company. It was a long hike down the muddy main road with dozens of hairpin bends, the jungle growing thicker and thicker near the recesses in the curves of the road, fed by the little watercourses that trickled down the hillside. I could smell death all the time, then I saw the fresh corpse of a Japanese soldier that had not been there the day before. I found his rifle first, on the road, and moved into the jungle to find his discarded pack, then his body. His head was hanging down over a stream. I wasn't sure he was dead at first and approached with care, but he was dead all right. The Japs' diet was mainly rice and they sometimes drank too much water, which caused the rice they'd eaten to swell and kill them. After throwing his rifle over the sheer drop into the bushy jungle beneath to prevent it being used again, I left the body where it was.

Our advance continued. At one location a muddy mound rose in the road. Stretchers, parts of an ambulance, skulls, helmets, bones and uniforms were all embedded in the mud, and our transport just drove over it, as our Company chased a retreating enemy who hadn't the time to clear the road properly or bury their dead. It was a sickly, awful sight. The mud was baked hard in places, with bits of body sticking out of it. A British bulldozer was called in some weeks later to do the job of clearing away the stinking mound of bodies, but meanwhile I had to climb over them.

I would deliver my messages to forward companies and try to get back to BHQ before it got dark. But I never did. It was always dark before I got as far as the 'mound of death'. I knew I was close by the smell, and although I had done this journey many times in the dark, I was always nervous. What it was about the place I don't know, but I always had my rifle ready with my finger on the trigger, prepared to blast any Jap I saw in front of me. It was a lonely road in the dark and I would be lucky to meet anyone on my runs. It was a very dangerous area, too; there were plenty of opportunities for the enemy to ambush me at every deep, jungle-covered curve and crevice in the dark corners of the mountain bends.

On top of all this, I had to remember the password when challenged by the guards at BHQ, hoping they would remember I was out there and not act trigger-happy. The guards would demand the password despite the fact that they knew it was me. They recognized my shape and voice, but used to pretend they hadn't heard. I would repeat the password, louder this time, but one of the guards would say, 'Speak louder next time'. It was a little game they played to break the monotonous hours of guard duty. They'd heard me fine the first time, and I'd swear at them as I passed through, while they laughed quietly. I couldn't do much about it. I couldn't blunder through without giving the password. They could have shot me.

I came across a part of the road that had dropped because of a landslide. About 100 yards of the road was gone. I had to climb over a slope of mud and shale and back on to the road again to take my messages to the forward positions. They got two bulldozers working on it, one from each end, and soon shaped a new road on the site of the landslide to get the traffic of war on the move once again. As my

Battalion advanced, the rain continued to pour down. The mud was so deep that it covered our boots, and lorries now found it difficult to keep a straight course, mindful of the sheer drop to the one side of the road. Ropes were used once again to stop the gun supports attached to the lorries going over the edge. You wouldn't get them back if they went; they'd be lost down the sheer drop in the jungle beneath.

Despite the weather, we could still hear the droning sound of the American Curtiss Commando and Dakota cargo planes dropping supplies further back. These would then be put on mules to carry up to us in the front line. We would have been at a loss without these planes and appreciated their support. They operated whatever the weather.

One day I left the road and climbed into the mountains following a track which led to a native Chin village. High on an outcrop of rocky land were stone-built huts with thatched roofs. They had no doors or windows, just rectangular openings. Nearby I noticed a tree with quite large fruit, like green-skinned oranges. I decided against going into this deserted village. It seeming too risky at the time, but I took half a dozen oranges, put them inside my tunic and continued to C Company's position further along the track. Here two badly wounded chaps were lying under a rough shelter with their stretchers off the ground. Both were well wrapped up and protected against the rain. They would need mules to get them out. It was a shame, and I wondered if they'd make it.

On my return journey I had to take some sick chaps back to BHQ. They weren't that bad and were mobile enough to travel unaided. One of the chaps was called Ingram and I knew him. I gave them some of my oranges to suck, cutting them in half, and although the fruit were sour and bitter they ate them. I didn't rush them and took a slow walk back, allowing them rest wherever possible. It was a dicey track if you were fit, let alone ill, and there were lots of stray Japs about. As we moved back, I was not too happy about that deserted Chin village with the orange tree. I made them rest for a few minutes while I scouted around the two dangerous bends in the track that could hide an ambush. Then I left them, entered the jungle and worked my way round the back, to check no one was lying in wait. All was clear, and we slowly went forward, down the open track on the mountainside to BHQ. After the war I met Ingram in Rangoon.

He always told others, 'Here's the chap who saved my life when I had typhus on the Imphal Road'. I would get quite embarrassed.

C Company was on the move again, and along the road we found an old out-of-action Jap tank. It had been pushed half way over the drop at the edge of the road. Further on, a Jap gun stood idle on some flat ground, its long barrel blown to pieces, sabotaged by the enemy so it couldn't be used against them. The smell of death was still with us and more dead Japs littered both sides of the road, some of their bodies partly buried in the mud. It was a vile sight; the debris of war was everywhere. We even found a lorry containing a money-printing machine and thousands of 'Japanese Rupee' notes with 'The Government of Japan' written on them. I collected a few clean ones to take home as souvenirs.

It was now nearly September. We moved forward, climbing higher. There was still heavy rain. My runs to C Company and back went on, each one becoming longer. When I got the chance I would explore Jap lorries abandoned along the road, searching for anything of interest, such as information or the odd souvenir. I never found anything worth keeping.

They were a good lot of chaps, our lot. We all mixed in together, the Cockneys, the Welsh and the rest. There was a lad with us called Bernard James, who spent most of his time with his two mates. He was only shot in the knee, but still died; he went into shock and never recovered. We couldn't believe he'd gone through the Arakan, Kohima and the rest, then died of shock! Some time later I was coming back from taking a message and I found a cross marking James' grave. Thinking I was alone, I picked some flowers, laid them by the cross and stood there for a little while. Then a voice said, 'Hello, Street'. It was the padre. I felt embarrassed. I don't know where he came from. We were in the middle of nowhere.

Eventually, our next objective, the 'Chocolate Staircase', came into sight, its winding hairpin bends climbing up the mountainside like steps. The chocolate-coloured mud covered everything, right up to the peak. We had some miles to go yet, though, and halted for a rest before we started to climb the road up the 'Staircase'. The weather got drier, with hot sunshine. We could clearly see the endless ranges of mountains disappearing away in the distance. I was detailed to take another run to my Company, now in front line mountain positions. On the way, I spotted a Jap half-track vehicle burnt out. There were no bodies in it, and I had a look inside. I found a pistol and leather holster attached to a bulletproof steel side panel and took it out for a look. It was a Luger style of pistol or automatic, but too badly burnt to keep as a souvenir, so I left it. Passing through the jungle, I began to notice that the water was drying up in the clear little mountain streams that ran from the jungle-covered crevices in the loops and bends of the road. It looked like the dry weather was here to stay.

We all marched up the Chocolate Staircase, the other traffic and guns moving up in lorries and on mules, passing some Indian troops moving down. We didn't know where they were going, but there was a lot of movement of troops going on at that time. During our march we would look out for water supply points along the road, hoping to see or hear some running water. I went down off the road into the thick cover of the jungle and found a wild banana grove, where I heard water running. Banana groves were a good clue, their large leaves would stand out and show that water was around, in this case 200 yards away down the mountainside. I made a mental note of the place as we marched past. We were now beginning to learn the ways of the jungle.

High up on this mountain we found a site to rest for the coming night. I was detailed to take a mule and another soldier back down to fill the water tanks. We retraced our steps down the road overlooking the banana grove. We moved carefully over rough, rocky areas between the bushes and trees and arrived amongst the banana trees growing out of a limestone ledge. There was our water supply, pouring into shallow pools about two or three inches deep on a bed of limestone. The place stank. Wild pigs had been foraging here, feeding off the rotting bananas and vegetation and churning everything up into a stinking mess. It didn't matter. We slowly filled the water tanks and bottles and returned with the mule to our position before darkness set in.

New orders now arrived. We were to go back down the Chocolate Staircase to the main road, take another route and infiltrate 80 miles behind the Japanese lines. This was a covert operation, and we left the road on a little-used track which led through mountains, valleys, native villages and open countryside. We met up with groups of natives and soldiers who had operated behind the Jap lines. Some had worked before the war as tea planters. We were going to give the Japs a shock in the days ahead as we'd brought in a battery of mountain guns on the mules, together with skilled Indian mountain battery gunners and their officers.

The retreating Japs intended to make a stand at a high point on the road beyond Tiddim called Kennedy Peak, where they would have a good view of our oncoming troops. If they could hold us here, it was said that this would give the rest of the Jap forces more time to make the next major river crossing, of the Chindwin River about 40 miles further east into Burma. There they could organize air transport and supplies, and it would give them time to clear their stores and regroup on the other side. Our job was to cut the road east of Kennedy Peak and trap as many of the Japs as possible. We marched at night under the relative safety of darkness and holed up in the daytime, in places close to the Japanese positions. The heat was unrelenting as we pushed forward, unloading the mules before first light, digging in and then trying to get some sleep between stints of guard duty. The noise of the insects and jungle creatures made sleeping difficult, but we got a little. In the late afternoon we would reload the mules and then be on the march again in the early evening.

We passed through many Chin villages, with their typical houses on stilts and decorated with buffalo horns. This was unusual to us, but one house that belonged to a Catholic priest stood out from the rest; it had an English-style lawn with a water tap. It was a real surprise to us, finding something like that in the middle of the mountains.

We continued marching, night after night. In places, some of the hillside tracks were so narrow the mules would scrape their loads against the cliff face, and they became nervous of the sheer drop on the other side. They would kick and buck as the muleteers struggled to control them. Because the animals were chained together in threes, if one bucked it was likely all three would become upset, kicking out in an attempt to lose their load. Indeed, on one occasion we actually lost three mules. The lead mule panicked, bucked and fell over the side, dragging the other two with it. We all watched in horror as the helpless creatures plunged down into the darkness. A group of soldiers and muleteers were sent to retrieve what they could and returned with some the loads that could be used, but the poor mules perished.

We pushed on higher and higher up the mountains, realizing that now the only way was forward. It was on this march that I tripped over a small rock on the track and this catapulted me over and down off the side of the road. Fortunately, I didn't fall too far, but I was carrying a full pack and equipment, and the sudden jolt winded me for a while. I got up and continued, but never seemed to be up to the pace after that.

One night, at the head of our long line of men, amongst the high ridges of pine forest that flanked the track, our CO and HQ Company Officer stopped to look at the maps more closely with their pencil torch. We had apparently come too far and were now in a very dangerous area. The order to halt came, BHQ and HQ Company moved on to the wooded ridges to the left of the mountain track and we started back. On the way, we came across a British officer with Indian tribal soldiers, working to make the mountain track wide enough to take jeeps. It was incredible to find them operating in this dangerous 'no-man's-land'. Nearby, we noticed the dead body of a Jap, only a few days old, sprawled over some bushes. We moved on past him and left the working party to get on with their job.

We holed up in a pine forest for a few days to do the job we were there for, but things didn't go to plan. The Japs soon discovered we were behind them. They tried to make a stand to delay us and we soon found that there were many more Japs and much more of their transport retreating down the Tiddim Road than we had realized. This was more than our small group of men could handle. We were only sent to mine the road, blow up lorries and then return to base. We went back to BHQ, dug in near the track with our rifle company flanking us and C Company to the rear, a few hundred yards back, and awaited further orders.

My runs were now sometimes twice a day, taking messages to and from my Company. I would go out in the late afternoon and return in darkness. It wasn't like previous runs. This time I was 80 miles behind the Jap lines, in virgin forest, and I had to find my own way back to BHQ in the pitch black. That was really hard up there in the pine forest. There were no proper tracks, and any that did exist had been made by us. It was all right during the day as I could recognize trees and shapes or surrounding high and low points, but in the darkness it was impossible. I only just about made it back the first time, after going into a small clearing in the forest to get a better idea of direction. It was more by luck than judgement that I came into an open area with fewer trees and found BHQ. I had been lost.

Fortunately, on leave I had bought a bone-handled Gurkha knife, suitable for cutting saplings or for use as a weapon. It came in very handy as I took my message the next day. I moved into the forest a few yards and blazed a new trail – but not a trail for daylight use, as a Jap patrol could then follow it to our camp. So I missed the first few trees, then I went behind a tree trunk and took a slice out, going down about a foot and leaving a light patch. I missed out a further three trees then repeated this several times, until I reached a small clearing. (This was another reminder of the comics I used to read as a kid about the old Wild West: the frontier folk cutting trails into the unknown). Almost out of the forest and into open land, with a few pines marked up near my Company position, I delivered the message. When it got dark, I re-entered the wood in the same place. Leaving the small clearing, I found the first blazed tree and retraced my tracks back to camp. It wasn't easy – I found it difficult having to go back to the marked trees to get my directions – but I eventually arrived at our camp and was passed through by the guard. By my third night I managed to make my way back in the dark quite easily, finding the marked trees a lot more quickly.

We felt our positions must be very close to the road south from Tiddim, as there were telephone poles and wire near our camp. We were ordered to cut those wires leading to the Jap lines and half a dozen of us set off, including some signallers, with a pair of pincers. They supplied each of us with pistols so we left our rifles behind to travel light and set off for a telegraph pole in a hollow on the forest floor overlooked by high ridges all around. One of the chaps went up the telegraph pole, only to find the wire was half an inch thick. It was hard going cutting it with the small pincers and seemed to take forever. As we finished we saw a patrol high on a ridge above. It was too far away to see who they were so we took cover behind some trees and got our pistols at the ready to fire. If they were enemy, they would be out of pistol range, but we would be within the range of their rifles. As they got closer we were relieved to see that they were ours. We got a surprise when they told us that we would have been dead ten minutes earlier if they had been the enemy. They had been watching us as we cut the telephone wire.

It was now nearly October and there was a kind of winter here on these high peaks. We stood to in our slit trench in a foggy, cold morning mist. We heard the heavy explosions of Jap shells somewhere in the valley below. We couldn't see anything because of the mist. If they were aiming at us they were well off target, and we were thankful that they couldn't see us. The shelling ceased and we heard no more. Our front rifle companies had made contact with the Japs and we heard the battle going on as our mountain guns opened fire in support. The noise soon quietened and we remained where we were. The next day we made our way down to the road on to some flat land and camped near a river by an old enemy position. There were some Jap graves with marker posts in wood and Japanese writing on them. Nearby, a small river ran over a gravel bed, and I decided to have a quick wash.

I found a lump in my left side and went to see the MO. I'd got a hernia, probably when I fell off the track, half asleep with exhaustion, during our march further back up in the mountains. Nothing could be done where we were. I needed surgery but I couldn't leave for hospital, as the nearest airstrip was still to be captured. We marched on for a few hours then camped in a teak forest near a former Jap base camp. We rested in our tents, and BHQ was set up near the sandy track. I noticed that the large trunks of the tall teak trees had no low branches and remember thinking that this was just as well, as I noticed a python hanging from one of the higher boughs! We pitched our tent near this tree, since the snake was well out of the way up there. However, in the fine sandy tracks around were a mass of snake trails of all sizes. Most of the snakes were small. We hoped they weren't poisonous, as to be bitten out here would probably be fatal. This reminded me of a four-foot-long grass snake with a bright red head that had surprised me up in the mountains. The snake came out of the bushes and slithered under a tent wall, and I happened to see it as I cleared some ground nearby. I dashed round the other side and cut its head off with one swing of my spade. I found out later that it was harmless and felt quite guilty for killing the poor reptile. I don't know whether this feeling was because we were constantly surrounded by death. We'd happily shoot the Japs. We had to. But it seemed unnecessary to kill animals for the sake of it.

While we were at this former Japanese camp I took the opportunity to look round. The NCO reminded me to watch out as there might still be some Jap stragglers hanging about in the jungle around, so I remained cautious. I saw two natives loading their bullock cart with some of the stores that the enemy had left behind. The cart was full and one of them was on the cart, the other nearby. They looked very worried but I thought they looked Burmese. Their hands were under their gowns. I couldn't see if they had any weapons. My rifle was slung over my shoulder, so I had the choice of either playing it cool and taking no notice or un-slinging my rifle and risking being killed before capturing them. I decided to play it cool and let them go on their way, but continued to look round. The other native quickly jumped on to the cart and they whipped the two bullocks and raced away. I could have shot them for looting, but there was no need. Good luck to them, I thought.

As I looked round I also saw some broken Jap rifles amongst the debris and tried to find one that would work. Looking more closely, I saw some half buried paper and gently dug it out. Someone had hidden it in a hurry. It turned out to be two military Japanese maps. They were beautifully coloured, showing the sea and coastline of either Burma or China, with neat Japanese writing. They were two feet wide, so I carefully folded them up, put them into my pocket and later handed them in to the Intelligence Officer. I found a rifle not damaged except for a missing bolt and a barrel packed with mud. Nearby, some leather pouches of Jap rifle bullets were tipped out on the ground. I got a bolt from another damaged rifle and loaded the weapon, cleared the rifle barrel with a bullet and moved into the forest to try it out. I fired a few shots at various targets before realizing that the noise of an enemy rifle might attract others, so I returned to camp.

Chapter 10

Hospital, Home, Back to Burma, Demob

In October 1944 a nearby Japanese airstrip was captured, so I waited for pay parade and went sick the next day, reporting my hernia. Arrangements were made, and I was flown to Imphal for treatment. The hospital at Imphal was a large tented camp, but wounded men and urgent cases took priority, so it was decided I would be treated elsewhere. After a week I was flown to a hospital in Chittagong, a coastal town on the Bay of Bengal. There I spent a further two weeks of relaxation and rest on the sandy beaches nearby, swimming in the warm sea. That was welcome. Eventually, I was taken by hospital ship to Madras and had my operation just before Christmas.

At that time a commemorative service was held back at Kohima. Some of the Royal West Kents were on the guard of honour. A mate of mine, Ronnie Millward, was there and had his photo taken. His family ran a business as sign writers and decorators. He was a great kid, and we used to get him to write letters to our girlfriends because he had such neat and stylish handwriting. Padre Randolph took the service, and that was apt; he was a tremendous spiritual support to those that needed it (there weren't many that didn't) when we were at Kohima. A teak cross was erected as a memorial. Ivan Daunt and Ernie Stonnell made it. They were sent to Dimapur after the Siege to choose some teak and spent hours inscribing all the dead men's names on it. It stood there for nearly twenty years before being brought back in pieces to England in 1961. Bob Clinch, a Pioneer sergeant of HQ Company, meticulously restored it, and it now is displayed in the Royal West Kent Museum in Maidstone.

Whilst recovering in hospital I contracted dysentery and malaria. It seemed ironic that I would nearly die of disease after surviving the battles of the Arakan, Kohima and the Imphal Road. We had lost many soldiers through the various tropical diseases, but fortunately I pulled through.

In January 1945 Lady Mountbatten visited the hospital. I had only recently had my operation and was lying flat on my back. I hoped she'd pass me by, but the nurse or someone must have said I was a member of the 4th Battalion of the Royal West Kents, back from the actions of Kohima and the Imphal Road. She made a beeline for me. I wanted to sink through the floor rather than meet her, but she smiled and chatted with me, asking if I had seen her husband. He was Lord Mountbatten, Supreme Allied Commander South-East Asia Command. I said that I had, but told her that every time we saw him, we went back into action. She went on to tell me how Lord Mountbatten thought the world of us and appreciated all the good work we'd done. Wishing me well and to get better soon, she passed on to chat to others. Several days later, the ward sister told me that someone had been asking about me; when I asked who it was, she said she was not allowed to say, but that they were very important. Anyway, she brought me a form to fill in and I was given special leave for a month in England.

I had to wait several weeks before being discharged from that hospital. In April 1945 I was sent to a convalescence depot in the Wellington Hills near Madras. After a couple of weeks of taking it easy and doing light duties such as laying tables, I was told by the NCO that my leave had come through. He added that when I was fit and ready to travel I could take my one month's home leave. He also said I could be downgraded and take an easier job when I returned. When the time came, it took me seventeen days to get back to England.

Arriving home was traumatic. At a family gathering I began to feel so strange; everything seemed unreal and my parents appeared to have grown old and grey since I saw them last. Things became confused and I burst into tears. After a few minutes I was all right again, but it seemed that the pressures of the last few months had finally surfaced. My mother got in touch with the local MP to complain that I was not fit enough to return to the front line. They even got an Army MO to check me over, but he said it was too late for him to do anything about it. He said that I should speak to someone when I got back, to arrange for a downgrade and an easier job in India, rather than going back to the front line. I wasn't bothered, but my mother was.

I remember one occasion while I was on home leave. I was on a bus with one of my aunts, laughing and joking. A woman came across to say I shouldn't be acting like I was – there was a war on and I should be out there fighting. Well, before I knew what was going on, my aunt reared up on her and gave her such a dressing down, telling her where I had been and what I had been through. I ended up having to separate the pair of them.

VE Day took place whilst I was in England, but my leave still ended all too quickly and I went by train to Glasgow to catch the troopship *Queen of Bermuda* back to Bombay. It was horrible when the train started to leave the station. Husbands had just parted from their wives and children in tearful farewells. Some of the poor blokes couldn't bring themselves to speak for a half hour or so. Others were virtually in tears. We single men left them to thaw out, joking and messing about, talking about our leave and playing cards. The others eventually joined in when they were ready.

In Bombay a mix-up took place, and instead of being given a soft job I was sent back to Calcutta and on to Rangoon, to the front line. It was my own fault, really. All the soldiers were lined up waiting to go back to their units, when a sergeant asked me which regiment I was from. I felt I couldn't say that I ought to be going to a convalescence depot, be downgraded and given an easy job. Not in front of all these other blokes. So I said I was with the Royal West Kents, hoping I would get a chance to sort it all out later; but I didn't. In a way, though, I was glad to be back in India, feeling somewhat free and enjoying the respect I received from the locals. It was as if I had gone back in time a thousand years. Bullock carts trundled along, high pitched music and singing wailed all around, a sacred cow chewed aimlessly. I loved it. This was my type of life, in this hot, dusty climate. Not like at home. Here people would rush to carry your bag, shine your shoes or sell you fruit and tea, and it all cost virtually nothing. Even the prospect of an uncertain future seemed part of the adventure. It was confusing; I couldn't wait to get home to England, but then I wanted the freedom and lifestyle we had out here in India. It was strange. Anyway, we were sent to Calcutta, then took ship across the Bay of Bengal to Rangoon to go back to the front line in Burma.

I hadn't been to Rangoon before – the city hadn't long been taken. When we got there my old Signals Sergeant met us. He was one of the old members of the West Kents and he'd served in the Middle East before coming to the Arakan. He was at Kohima in the Signals Bunker just a few yards higher than our trench and had served in the front line throughout the months I had been away in hospital and on home leave. He said it would be too risky to return to my Company that night, so we had a night on the town in Rangoon.

We took the opportunity to visit the sights. One of these was the Shwedagon Pagoda, a vast complex, with hundreds of Buddhas sitting and lying in small temples. It was night, and we soldiers wandered round as a group. We could see the priests in their saffron robes, their heads shaved, attending the candlelit shrines. I lit a candle, made my wish and gave the candle to a young Burmese woman with white flowers in her hair. With thoughts of impending action, I wished I was home again. After our visit to the pagoda we went to a Chinese restaurant for a meal of lobsters, large prawns, salad and coffee.

The next day, our sergeant drove us very fast out of Rangoon, as there were Jap snipers about. We followed the tarmac main road, passing through flooded paddy fields on either side, driving through monsoon rain broken only by short periods of hot sunshine. As we travelled, we could see clusters of palm trees around villages, with people tending their water buffaloes. In the distance I could hear the faint sound of gunfire and began to tense up with that feeling of dread I had experienced before. I knew it would pass when I'd got used to being in action again, but it didn't help at the time. We passed through wayside villages of huts on stilts, one even with an open front selling fruit, an amazing sight. Eventually, we arrived at BHQ, a tented site in a sea of watery mud. It was gloomy place, but thankfully someone else had got my job as runner. I returned to my C Company in another village of huts on stilts, where I was allotted a hut with some people I knew from the old days, but also noticed quite a number of new young lads.

They filled me in on what was happening. They had been patrolling a 20-mile sector to clear a few Japs still left in the local area after the race to capture Rangoon in the past days. The main road was still unsafe to use. Just before I'd arrived, a lorry taking some soldiers back to Rangoon to catch a troopship to England had been ambushed. Several of the men were killed. Now back in a platoon of C Company, I joined one of these Jap clearing patrols, but luckily only did a couple of sorties before we moved on.

We were transported to the area we were to patrol, thus reducing the marching we had done in previous campaigns. We still had to cross the flooded paddy fields, however. Some were now drying out, but others had streams flowing through them. We stored our cigarettes and matches in our steel helmets as we waded across. I pitied the non-swimmers and very short people. The water was at least waist-deep and rose slowly to our chests and above before we passed the deepest point and climbed out on the other side. As we approached the villages on higher, drier ground, about a dozen water buffalo with vast, sweeping horns lowered their heads and turned towards us, getting ready to charge. We continued to approach, our lives (or rather the lives of these buffaloes) depending on a ten-year-old Burmese lad in charge of them. All he had was a catapult that fired clay marbles. The buffaloes began to form a half-circle and moved forward as if to charge. We stood our ground, our rifles and automatic weapons at the ready, at about 100 yards. The young lad saw the danger and started shouting at the buffaloes. At the same time he fired clay marbles from his catapult at them to try to stop the charge. It worked, saving the animals' lives and perhaps the village food supply, too.

We moved forward and checked out the village for Japs. There didn't appear to be any, and the villagers said that there were no Japs in the area. We carried on with our patrol, meeting up with some trucks at the pick-up point on the road, then returning to our base. A large clay urn about four feet high lay on its side outside our hut. Seeing that it could store plenty of water, we placed it under the eaves of the pitched thatch roof of our hut. As the waves of monsoon rain fell, the large urn soon filled past overflowing. We took full advantage and filled our water bottles, washed out our mess tins, washed down our bodies and had a shave. We stayed in the village for several days, and I had noticed that some of the huts were empty so went to have a look around. In one I found a roughly made crossbow, but it was broken. I repaired it with a piece of signal wire, used a six-inch nail for a bolt and fired it at a nearby tree. The nail buried itself about an inch into the trunk, and it was difficult to get out. I messed around a little longer with my new toy and then went back to base.

Some days later O (Operations) Group called, and we were given the job of blocking the escape routes of several thousand Japs trapped in the Pegu Yomas hills. They were dying of disease and starvation and preparing to try to break out towards the Siam border, across a main road where we were positioned. We moved towards Pegu by jeep-train (a jeep pulling flat-top trucks) to a railway embankment overlooking a track to the main road. We dug in on the embankment and could see across the flooded paddy fields, with a village in the background, to one of the escape tracks the Japanese might use to reach Siam – or die of disease or starvation in the low, jungle-covered hills of the Pegu Yomas. It was our job to patrol along this track and tackle any leading groups of Japs that had started to move out from the main body. As we climbed into the flat-top trucks I put on a new bush hat to protect me from the sun, but out on the paddy fields a gust of wind blew it off. So it was back to the steel helmet.

We lived in the open, rain or shine, spending day and night in our trenches, while we remained in position to block these escape routes. At the bottom of the railway embankment was a paddy field, flooded and full of weeds, fish and frogs. I wasn't happy with this position. I thought it would limit the use of grenades if the Japs attacked out of the paddy. This would be a battle for the Bren, rifle and bayonet. We were told we could call on the support of the air strikes, tanks and artillery at our rear, if required. I decided to take things a little further and put out 'pungies' – short lengths of bamboo stake hidden in the two-foot-high grass. I positioned them at a forty-five degree angle, sticking about six inches out of the ground and with trip-wires concealed amongst them. This was to try to stop any attacking Japs surprising me in the night. If they did come they'd trip and fall on to the pungies, giving me a chance to shoot first.

After two nights on guard we heard splashes in the water of the paddy field, and the croaking frogs suddenly fell silent. All was quiet for about five minutes as I strained my eyes, rifle and fixed bayonet ready to beat off any attack. Then the frogs started up once more, calling to their mates; we were safe again for the time being. This went on night after night. It was an awful feeling, when the frogs and other creatures suddenly went quiet. We stayed very much alert, but the enemy never came.

One day we were needed for a fighting patrol. An officer led out a full platoon of about twenty men, including me. Information had been received that a Gurkha patrol had clashed with a large number of Japs, who had retreated back down a track. The Gurkhas had suffered some wounded and killed. It was thought the Japs would attempt a breakout here, so they decided to send a fighting patrol from our Company to check it out. We moved out in single file, no talking, passing through the village out into open paddy fields, then on to a track through six-foot-high reeds and marsh grass. We remained alert and moved ever slower, our weapons at the ready. Sections spread out either side of the track ready for action, but none came.

Later, we heard shouting and the crashing of many feet coming in our direction, but we couldn't see anything through the high screen of reeds and grass. On the left hand side of the track our officer signalled to us to halt, and we spaced out and took up positions of defence. The enemy seemed to be just yards away behind the reeds. We had our safety catches forward and were ready to fire. Then, about ten yards in front of our officer, the leader of a large herd of cattle smashed down the tall reeds and high grass to cross the track, disappearing into the vegetation on the other side. Behind were the rest of the herd with the drover still shouting at them in Burmese. They didn't notice us. We covered a further mile or so to open paddy fields and then had come far enough. It was time to go back, and we returned along the same track to base.

A day or two later, we were detailed to take over from others on a standing patrol, just watching and listening. This meant listening to the dogs on the other side of the village we were in, in front of our defensive position. We were not sure why they were barking – perhaps it was because there was a group of Japs in that part of the village? A village woman offered us some tea without milk or sugar in a saucer-like bowl. We accepted thankfully and gave her some cigarettes. She liked that. It was a change from the thick type of cigar that most old Burmese women seemed to smoke. Later, we did a little trading of fresh eggs for a few tins of our sardines.

After a few more patrols around the Pegu area we returned to Rangoon. There was talk of sending us in gliders to attack some guns on the coast near the Malayan border, but we were given a job in Rangoon for a couple of weeks, looking after Japanese prisoners of war at the local jail. We felt like prisoners ourselves, locked in that Wild-West-style courtyard with a lot of Japs and iron bars all around. It wasn't easy guarding the prisoners. We were always on edge. We had been fighting these people and they were still our enemy. We were allowed to smoke and as we did so the Jap prisoners shuffled around and waited for us to throw away the nub-ends. Then they would move forward, point to the cigarette end on the ground and hiss like a snake whilst standing to attention, bowing all the time, until we gave them permission to pick it up. I would let them and again they bowed and hissed until I waved them away. Some soldiers were not as soft as me and would simply put their foot on the cigarette, raise a rifle towards the prisoners and send them on their way with a volley of verbal abuse.

Once I had to escort a Jap officer to the cookhouse. He spoke good English and had a good sense of humour. However, when we reached the cookhouse his voice suddenly changed and he bellowed out orders, sounding like some sort of wild animal. It shocked me. He was tall, and the smaller Japs ran round doing as he said. They brought him some rice cakes and he calmly and politely offered me one. They looked and smelled good, but I couldn't eat with him and refused. I didn't mind talking but I wasn't going to share his food. He was upset, but as far as I was concerned he was the enemy and we were still at war. You don't eat with your enemies and that was that.

In August 1945 we heard the Americans had dropped the atom

bomb and we were told the war would be over soon. We didn't count our chickens. We were used to that kind of talk and carried on as usual. Off duty, we wandered around Rangoon and took in the sights. We were on our way back from the Chinese quarter after a meal when we heard a lot of noise and shooting. In all the commotion I thought the Japs had counter-attacked. Then we saw a jeep with some officers firing their pistols into the air. They were shouting and cheering, saying that the Japs had surrendered. When we got back to the jail we told the prisoners the news. They didn't believe us at first and shouted all sorts of abuse. Finally, they realized it was true and became scared of what was to happen to them. They needn't have worried; our treatment was far better than what they gave our chaps, as we realized when we saw some of our men at the docks waiting for the boat home. They were in a dreadful state and were really shocked and upset to hear how well we had treated enemy prisoners. But we couldn't take retribution; it wasn't our place to do so.

Around Christmas 1945 we were detailed to oversee the local Rangoon dockworkers (or coolies, as we called them). They were loading and unloading the boats at the harbour, and it was our job to see that everything went where it was supposed to and that nothing went missing. We were allowed to keep any damaged fruit tins and often opened and helped ourselves to these perks. Unfortunately, I ate a dodgy tin of pears and caught a tapeworm. I first noticed the end of it still wriggling in some of the fruit I had just swallowed. I immediately threw the rest away. The MO was not that sympathetic and gave me a dressing-down for not keeping the rest of the pears. He said that if I'd done so, he would have been able to identify the sex of the tapeworm, to see if it could breed inside me. I hadn't and so was hospitalized for nearly two weeks, to clear my system.

The war had ended, but we didn't go home straight away. Things still had to be sorted out. We had to wait our turn. Anyway, I'd signed up until 1949. I can't think of anything worse than to have survived that lot and then be killed later on, but that happened to some. For example, Dick Pooley stepped on a mine in Rangoon. He had joined up in 1939, served in Africa and the Middle East as well as Burma, fighting the Germans and Italians as well as the Japs. What a way to go after all that. I wouldn't let that happen to me.

Soon after leaving hospital, I was detailed with others to track down bandits until some semblance of order and discipline returned to the country. Although the job was still difficult, the pressure was not great, and during rest periods some of the men would fish in the ponds that the locals had behind their huts. Some chaps even had Burmese girlfriends and they weren't at all pleased when it was time to move on, preferring to stay rather than go home.

In 1946 my one month's home leave came through. I returned to England on board the *Stamford Victory*. Some days after leaving Gibraltar, a cool breeze blew in our faces as we stood on the gun deck looking out to sea. We were in our thick battledress now. Someone pointed to some dark clouds on the horizon, shouting, 'There's England'.

We all laughed, saying it couldn't be England, it was just clouds.

'You'll see', he said.

And he was right. A few hours later, Southampton was in plain view. As we approached, I had mixed feelings. Things were confusing and unreal after all that had happened. As usual, the Army didn't give us time to think. The order came to parade and get ready to go ashore. Kit, kitbags and everything else had to be sorted out. As soon as we got ashore we boarded trains for home.

After my leave, I returned to duty at Maidstone Barracks; but after a few days I felt sick during dinner and threw my food away. The NCO put me on a charge for wasting it, but it didn't stick. Hours later, I was in a military hospital with malaria. Ten days later, I was a lot better and was sent to Kingston Convalescence Depot. However, shortly after eating a bag of black cherries, I awakened a germ from my jungle days and found myself with amoebic dysentery (the worst type) and was immediately re-hospitalized. When I recovered, I returned to Kingston Convalescence Depot and was discharged from the Army.

It was 1947. I travelled by train back to Birmingham and tried to make sense of what I'd been through. I didn't know what I was going to do in the future. Nobody gave us any advice. They left us to it. I thought of all the chaps that didn't make it back. Friends had been wounded, and I didn't know if they were still alive. That was upsetting. I thought of Company Sergeant Major Haines, who was blinded at Kohima and continued to fight and encourage his men whilst guided round the front line by a private. I thought of Jack Harman and others like him, and his heroic actions in winning the Victoria Cross during the Siege. His deeds no doubt saved many of us. I remembered that a memorial had been erected in Kohima to commemorate those that had died. It is still there and its inscription reads:

When you go home
Tell them of us and say
For your Tomorrow
We gave our Today

Postscript

by
Raymond Street

It was difficult for me in Birmingham after the war. Things weren't
the same. I found it hard to re-adjust, but I did. I was one of the lucky
ones – for many veterans it was hell, after what we'd all been
through. But you just had to get on with it. There wasn't any
counselling in those days. You were out of the Army and they left
you to it. I remember on one occasion hearing some fireworks going
off and diving flat on to the ground instinctively, as if under fire. The
girl I was with thought it was hilarious, but I was embarrassed. She
didn't understand, really. Shortly after coming home I met a nice Irish
girl who was lodging at my cousin's house. Her name was Ann.
Things seemed to be on the up, and we married in July 1947.

When I left the Army I was registered disabled because of all my
illnesses and could only get low paid jobs. I was supposed to only
do light work. The Army gave me a pension, but that was only twelve
shillings a week. However, I was married now and needed to earn
more money. It was the end of 1947 before I got my first job, in an
upholstery warehouse, sorting out all the different springs. The wages
were only £5 a week. It was supposed to be easy work, but it wasn't.
We had our first baby in 1948, a little girl, Linda. She became poorly,
and I remember being at work one day and thinking that I heard Ann
scream my name. It was so clear that I looked round, but she wasn't
there. She was at home. Fifteen minutes later, the boss called me in.
He had received a phone call and sent me home. Linda had died of
pneumonia. It was awful. Even after what I had done and seen,
nothing could prepare me for that. It was a terrible feeling.

After a couple of years I couldn't stick at the job any longer, so
my mother set me up in a second-hand furniture shop. It had my name
over the door, but it was her shop, really. I did that until 1954 then

worked for the BRS (British Road Services), checking the loads on and off lorries. That was boring. Fortunately, I got a transfer to loading lorries. The money wasn't much better and the work was a lot harder, but I preferred it. We had three more children by then: another girl first (I was glad about that, especially for Ann), then two boys. I kept that job for nearly six years, but it didn't pay enough, not with a wife and three children to support. So in 1960 I passed my driving test and had another go at running a furniture shop. This time, though, it was to be my own, and I sold new furniture, not second-hand. I rented a shop in Camp Hill, near Birmingham city centre, and gave it a go. Things went well at first, and we soon moved out of my mother's house into our own. But it didn't last. The shop burned down in the mid-sixties, and I had to start again. It seemed that the luck I had had during the war had worn thin. The shop was rebuilt and I started again. Just as I got back on my feet, my luck deserted me again. Ann died in 1970 and I was left with the three children to bring up. Later that year, my daughter married. It was hard: the boys were still at school and I had to keep going for them. In 1979 I retired. The council had started to widen my road, and eventually, mine was the last building standing on it. I wasn't going to start all over again, so I packed up. Then my luck changed for the better: the boys left school and were working, I met Val and we married in 1981.

When I look back I consider myself lucky. I've had a good life, really. Yes, I've had hard times, but a lot of good times, too. I have seen the world, experienced and seen much more than some people could ever dream of. I have a lovely family, with nine grandchildren, and that's nice. I have more time to myself now. When I was younger I was too busy working, but now I can enjoy playing with the grandchildren. They often come to see us. I still talk about the war, even to them. They like that. I think it's important they know. Perhaps my telling them can help them to realize they shouldn't get involved, should another war start. Don't get me wrong, though, I wouldn't change it. Not the Arakan, Kohima, the Imphal Road, not a thing. I was proud to serve in the Royal West Kents and would do the same again. But now I want to enjoy my family and do my best for them. I also think it's about leaving a little something behind so they can better remember me. I think I've done that now.

Appendix A

4th Battalion of The Queen's Own Royal West Kent Regiment

Kohima Roll of Honour

Those who gave their lives during the
Siege of Kohima
from 5 April to 20 April 1944

Capt. J Topham
Lieut. G Inglis

CSM W G Haines, MM	Sgt. H G Chantler	Sgt. A H Crathern
Sgt. G F Boxwell	Sgt. L Peacock	L/Sgt. T H Morley
Sgt. W G Millichap	Cpl. E G Hatton	Cpl. A E Judge
Cpl. G Fidler	Cpl. G Martin	Cpl. L Rees
Cpl. W G S Moxworthy	Cpl. L W Rose	Cpl R F Bowles
Cpl. T Rees	Cpl. A W Want	L/C. G E Mann
L/C. J P Harman, VC	L/C. W H Hill	Pte. A T Hawker
Pte. A Hankinson	L/C. S King	Pte. S W Williams
Pte. F Worth	Pte. H V Allchin	Pte. G S Baker
Sgt. E H Bennett	Pte. G P Bloomfield	Pte. J J Brattman
Pte. J Bradstreet	Pte. D L Bunnell	Pte. R C Cook
Pte. J D Coleman	Pte. H A Collins	Pte. L S Collins
Pte. S F Calton	Pte. H J Crosbie	Pte. K R Davies
Pte. W D Davies	Pte. L C Fisher	Pte. P H Fall
Pte. W Forsyth	Pte. C A V Foord	Pte. C W Gray
Pte. A E Guilford	Pte. I W Gwilt	Pte. F W Gipps
Pte. F Hall	L/C. J A Hazell	Pte. J G Haslam
Pte. J K Hesketh	Pte. H T Hopkins	Pte. P Hughes
Pte. A G M Judges	Pte. G O Jones	Pte. C J Keating
Pte. D A M Mancey	Sgt. H A Norton	Pte. D Oliver
Pte. A Paris	Pte. S E Roberts	Pte. C E Roberson
Pte. C Sims	Pte. J Sinclair	Pte. C R Trussler
Pte. J P Walsh	Pte. R E Walters	Pte. E W Wells
Pte. S Weeks	Pte. D Windle	Pte. R Gartrell
Pte. C Williams	Pte. E B Whittingham	Pte. D J Jack
Pte. A Williams	Pte. J Williams	Pte. G H Stenner

Appendix B

After the Siege

The Battle of Kohima continued for several more weeks after the Siege. The 2nd Division first consolidated the Allied positions left by the defenders during the Siege. It then reoccupied the previously relinquished Allied areas, eventually pushing the Japanese even further back, until there was a general retreat from the Kohima area.

The Battle of Kohima, which had started when the Japanese arrived on 5 April 1944, was actually considered to be finally over on 6 June 1944 (coincidentally, D-Day in Europe).

The Japanese retreated from Kohima both south along the main Dimapur–Imphal Road and also south/south-east across country towards both Imphal (where the other Japanese advance had come to a standstill) and the Indo-Burmese border. The end result was a general Japanese retreat back into Burma. Kohima had been the first significant Japanese land defeat, and they were then continuously pushed eastwards until their eventual surrender in 1945.

For more details of the Battle of Kohima in all of its stages, the reader is referred to the very comprehensive account provided in *Kohima – The Furthest Battle* by Leslie Edwards, published by the History Press in 2009.